P9-CEG-986

The Life and Death of Carolina Maria de Jesus

 DIÁLOGOS

A SERIES OF COURSE-ADOPTION BOOKS ON LATIN AMERICA

Independence in Spanish America: Civil Wars, Revolutions, and Underdevelopment (revised edition)—Jay Kinsbruner, Queens College

Heroes on Horseback: A Life and Times of the Last Gaucho Caudillos—John Charles Chasteen, University of North Carolina at Chapel Hill

The Life and Death of Carolina Maria de Jesus—Robert M. Levine, University of Miami, and José Carlos Sebe Bom Meihy, University of São Paulo

The Countryside in Colonial Latin America—Edited by Louisa Schell Hoberman, University of Texas at Austin, and Susan Migden Socolow, Emory University

¡Que vivan los tamales! Food and the Making of Mexican Identity—Jeffrey M. Pilcher, The Citadel

The Faces of Honor: Sex, Shame, and Violence in Colonial Latin America—Edited by Lyman L. Johnson, University of North Carolina at Charlotte, and Sonya Lipsett-Rivera, Carleton University

The Century of U.S. Capitalism in Latin America—Thomas F. O'Brien, University of Houston

Tangled Destinies: Latin America and the United States—Don Coerver, Texas Christian University, and Linda Hall, University of New Mexico

Everyday Life and Politics in Nineteenth Century Mexico: Men, Women, and War— Mark Wasserman, Rutgers, The State University of New Jersey

Lives of the Bigamists: Marriage, Family, and Community in Colonial Mexico— Richard Boyer, Simon Fraser University

Andean Worlds: Indigenous History, Culture, and Consciousness Under Spanish Rule, 1532–1825— Kenneth J. Andrien, Ohio State University

The Mexican Revolution, 1910–1940—Michael J. Gonzales, Northern Illinois University

Quito 1599: City and Colony in Transition—Kris Lane, College of William and Mary

Argentina on the Couch: Psychiatry, State, and Society, 1880 to the Present—Edited by Mariano Plotkin, CONICET (National Council of Scientific Research, Argentina), and Universidad Nacional de Tres de Febrero, Buenos Aires, Argentina.

A Pest in the Land: New World Epidemics in a Global Perspective—Suzanne Austin Alchon, University of Delaware

The Silver King: The Remarkable Life of the Count of Regla in Colonial Mexico— Edith Boorstein Couturier, Ph.D., Professor Emerita

National Rhythms, African Roots: The Deep History of Latin American Popular Dance— John Charles Chasteen, University of North Carolina at Chapel Hill

The Great Festivals of Colonial Mexico City: Performing Power and Identity— Linda A. Curcio-Nagy, University of Nevada at Reno

The Souls of Purgatory: The Spiritual Diary of a Seventeenth-Century Afro-Peruvian Mystic, Ursula de Jesús—Nancy E. van Deusen, Western Washington University

Dutra's World: Wealth and Family in Nineteenth-Century Rio de Janeiro— Zephyr L. Frank, Stanford University

Death, Dismemberment, and Memory: Body Politics in Latin America—Edited by Lyman L. Johnson, University of North Carolina at Charlotte

Plaza of Sacrifices: Gender, Power, and Terror in 1968 Mexico—Elaine Carey, St. John's University

Women in the Crucible of Conquest: The Gendered Genesis of Spanish American Society, 1500–1600—Karen Vieira Powers, Arizona State University

Beyond Black and Red: African-Native Relations in Colonial Latin America— Edited by Matthew Restall, Pennsylvania State University, University Park

Mexico OtherWise: Modern Mexico in the Eyes of Foreign Observers—Edited and translated by Jürgen Buchenau, University of North Carolina at Charlotte

SERIES ADVISORY EDITOR: LYMAN L. JOHNSON, UNIVERSITY OF NORTH CAROLINA AT CHARLOTTE

The Life and Death of
CAROLINA MARIA DE JESUS

Robert M. Levine and
José Carlos Sebe Bom Meihy

University of New Mexico Press
Albuquerque

© 1995 by the University of New Mexico Press
All rights reserved. Published 1995
First edition

12 11 10 09 08   04 05 06 07 08

LIBRARY OF CONGRESS CATALOGING-IN-PUBLICATION DATA

Levine, Robert M.
The life and death of Carolina Maria de Jesus
Robert M. Levine and Jose Carlos Sebe Bom Meihy.—1st ed.
p.   cm.—(Diálogos) Includes index.
1. Jesus, Carolina Maria de.
2. Brazil—History—20th century.
3. Blacks—Brazil—Sao Paulo—Social conditions.
4. Sao Paulo (Brazil)—Social conditions.
5. Blacks—Brazil—Biography.
I. Meihy, Jose Carlos Sebe Bom, 1943–   . II Title.
III. Series: Diálogos (Albuquerque, New Mexico)
F2537.J47L48   1995
981'.61062'092—dc20
[B] 95-4352
CIP

ISBN 978-08263-1648-6

Dedication

To the grandchildren of Carolina Maria de Jesus:
José (Zé) Carlos de Jesus's Lilian, Eliane, Elisa, Adriana, Ana,
Jackson, and Jonas; Vera Eunice de Jesus Lima's Ricardo
Alexandre, Luciana Cristina, Marisa Regina, Paulo César.

and

In Memory of Alice de Camargo Bom Meihy

Contents

Illustrations

Audálio Dantas with Carolina at her shack, 1960. Courtesy Audálio Dantas.

Preface

This study of the life of Carolina Maria de Jesus (1914-1977) is the result of an unusual collaborative project involving Robert M. Levine of the University of Miami and Professor José Carlos Sebe Bom Meihy of the University of São Paulo (USP). The documentation includes eight original, in-depth interviews of persons close to the subject during her life, and excerpts from the original manuscripts of her autobiographical writing. Robert M. Levine wrote most of the text and translated from the Portuguese. He also designed the map. José Carlos Sebe supervised the field interviews and the Brazilian edition of this book and contributed to the analysis.

Carolina Maria de Jesus was a destitute black Brazilian woman born in the rural interior who migrated to São Paulo, the largest industrial city in Latin America, seeking to find work and a better life. She became literate on her own, having attended school for less than two years. As a young girl, she developed a passion for reading. Later, this fed her desire to write down her feelings and to tell her story. In 1958 a reporter, Audálio Dantas, discovered that she had written a diary about her hard life; he managed to edit it and have it printed. The book became a sensation, bringing her worldwide fame. She wrote four other books, which were published without success, and many poems, short stories, and memoir fragments. Only a few years after her mercurial success, however, she was forced back into poverty, and she died ignored. This study probes the reasons for this black author's meteoric rise and fall from public attention. It seeks not only to recover her memory, but to put that memory in a context that is at the same time historical, social, and cultural.

Our study uses not only Carolina Maria de Jesus's writings but materials found in newspaper archives, other conventional sources, and interviews with the eight persons close to her life tracked down by members of

the research team. It incorporates her published autobiographical work—
the trilogy *Diário de Bitita*, *Casa de Alvenaria*, and *Quarto de Despejo*—
as well as manuscript fragments from earlier drafts that were not published.
The interview subjects included Audálio Dantas; Paulo Dantas (not related to Audálio), her publisher; Maria Puerta, her best friend from the
favela; Marta Teresinha Godinho, her social worker; Cecília Maria da
Silva, the president of a woman's association named after Carolina Maria
de Jesus in Guarujá in the state of São Paulo, and Carolina's* surviving
children, Vera Eunice de Lima and José (Zé) Carlos de Jesus.

José Carlos Sebe Bom Meihy has fought for years to gain respect for
oral history in Brazilian academic circles, and in 1992 he helped found
Brazil's Oral History Association. José Carlos's approach is sometimes
called "life story" oral history. Subjects are informed about the goals of
the project—in our case, the life and legacy of Carolina Maria de Jesus—
and then encouraged to talk with as little further questioning or intervention as possible. The recorded statements are then transcribed, exactly as
they were given. Nothing is taken out: pauses, bad grammar, or anything
else. Then the transcript is typed and given to the interviewee to read.
The subject then meets with the interviewer and is given the opportunity
to make any changes in the transcript he or she wants, even if this means
taking out "good" material. The process forced us to consider the imbal-
ance of power in the interview relationship, hence our effort in this study
to reflect on our own values and subjectivities and to attempt to interfere
as little as possible.[1]

Student volunteers played an indispensable role in our project. First
and foremost was the leader of the group, Juliano Andrade Spyer. Other
important members were Janes Jorge, Andrea Paula dos Santos, Flávio
Edson de Souza Brito, Maria Eta Vieira, and Rodrigo de Freitas Balbi.
João Carlos Amoroso Botelho and Edson Dionísio de Souza Carvalho
also helped. Luis Gonzaga Ferreira mobilized the family of Dona Maria
Puerta, so that her interview turned out to be more broad-reaching than
originally expected. At the University of Rostock, Dr. Jens Hentschke
obtained invaluable publication data about the various German editions
of Carolina's work as well as on the royalty arrangements by which the

---

* *The name Carolina will be used interchangeably with her full name, Carolina
Maria de Jesus. This follows the Brazilian custom of using mainly a person's
first name, and does not convey disrespect in any way.*

German publishers acted as a subagency for Catalina W. de Wulff in Buenos Aires to publish her diary in German as *Tagebuch der Armut*. Shigeru Suzuki of the Tokyo University of Foreign Studies kindly researched the Japanese translation of Carolina's diary, even comparing the translation line by line to find omissions.

In Miami we want to acknowledge Cristina Mehrtens for her diligence and insight. We received invaluable assistance from specialists not only in the United States but in Europe and Brazil as well. These persons included Jane Collins, Anani Dzidzienyo, Sandra S. Fernandes Erickson, Thomas Holloway, Martha D. Huggins, Lyman L. Johnson, Mary D. Karasch, Bob Rose, Daphne Patai, Darlene Sadlier, Carmen Chaves Tesser, Steven C. Topik, and Rosângela Maria Vieira, all of whom read portions or all of the draft manuscript and commented. Tim Power assigned part of the manuscript to his Fall 1993 political science class at LSU and asked each of his students to write a paper analyzing Carolina's legacy and the reaction of Brazilian society to her. Elissa Jastal wrote her paper in the form of a "letter to Vera," which was sent to Vera Eunice to read. "Your mother," Elissa wrote, "was unable to find a physical space for herself in Brazil, however she did find a spiritual place for her mind in her diary." Luke O'Brien argued that the point of Carolina's diary should be to see the "rift [between rich and poor] and find a more reasonable way to deal with the problems associated with it. But as long as Latin American politicians worry about their own personal benefits, the economies continue to stagnate from too much foreign dependence, and continual political unrest within, the problems of the favelas will never be solved." Most students extended empathy to Carolina, although one wrote: "I do not believe [the book] belongs in our class. Politics is a realm dominated by the elite and therefore the elite should be studied."

Megan Challinor, Jenny Pilling, and Gerald Curtis provided translation assistance, although Robert M. Levine and José Carlos Sebe Bom Meihy take responsibility for accuracy. We also contacted members of the Internet network, asking questions about how well Carolina Maria de Jesus and her writing is known today, and received some very interesting replies. Janaína Amado of the University of Brasília and her husband Luis also provided thoughtful feedback. An earlier version of Carolina's story appeared as an occasional paper in the series produced by the Helen Kellogg Center at the University of Notre Dame and in the *Latin Ameri-*

can Research Review. A different version of the book, emphasizing to a much greater extent the political context of the period in which Carolina Maria de Jesus lived, was published in Brazil in 1994 by the Federal University of Rio de Janeiro's press.[2]

Readers not familiar with Brazilian racial terminology should note that, as in the United States, the word *white* connotes a person of Caucasian ancestry, although in Brazil racial identity historically has been based as much on economic status as on racial lineage. *Black* in the United States means anyone with known African (or Negroid) ancestry, including light-skinned persons of mixed-race background. In Brazil, *black* is used only for persons of very dark skin. A considerable number of other terms are used to describe persons of intermediary mixtures, including *mulatos* (persons with mostly African and Caucasian ancestry) and *caboclos* (persons of mixed Amerindian, African, and Caucasian origin).

The Life and Death of Carolina Maria de Jesus

1
Introduction

The project that resulted in this book only came about after intense conversations between the co-authors over the importance of Carolina Maria de Jesus as a symbol of the Brazilian condition. Initially, José Carlos Sebe balked, conveying his frustration at the fact that so many foreign specialists on Brazil year after year used her translated diary in their classes. Over time, both authors came to regard the viewpoint of the other, setting out to look farther into aspects of Carolina's life to reveal not only her story but what it explains about Brazilian society's attitudes toward race, poverty, and gender. Although the authors are male, each respects the admonition that biographers of women have the responsibility "to understand both their subjects' cultures and their own and to provide their readers with a bridge back into history, so that they understand why certain behaviors then were approved or disapproved."[1] We appreciate that at times a woman's narrative becomes a different story when told in the voice of male biographers, but we have attempted to avoid distortion.

This is how the authors explain their relationship to the subject of this book:

Robert M. Levine

My introduction to favelas and their inhabitants came when I was a graduate student in Rio de Janeiro carrying out research for my dissertation on the political and ideological underpinnings of the presidency of Getúlio Vargas during the 1930s. One of the more arresting events I re-

Artwork by Teobaldo Dias de [dos] Santos, 1964. Robert M. Levine collection.

member most about my fifteen-month stay during 1964–65 was a small black crippled boy crouched on the pavement in front of one of the movie theaters on Avenida Nossa Senhora de Copacabana near Posto 6. He was drawing pictures in ink with a brush on white cardboard, selling them for a few cents to passers-by. I liked his work, purchased one, and returned the following week to buy another for a gift. This time he drew a picture of a favela, with a boy and girl at the bottom, holding a flower. He wrote on the bottom of each of his drawings "by Teobaldo Dias de [dos] Santos, ten years old." I spoke with several Brazilians about the possibility of organizing a group of sponsors who might pay for him to go to school, perhaps to study art, and give him medical treatment. Everyone I spoke to about the idea, however, declined, saying (sometimes with gratuitous hostility) that if we gave him money it would likely be snatched away by the adult who was paying for his supplies and taking away his proceeds at the end of the day. The upper-middle class Brazilians I knew clearly were not interested in favela-dwellers or their problems.

I returned to the United States to complete my dissertation and began teaching Latin American history at the State University of New York at Stony Brook. Although I had long been aware of poverty in the U.S., I had never closely observed destitution that even approached the stomach-turning hopelessness that I had seen close up in Brazil. I remember as a teenager riding the Long Island Railroad from the south shore of suburban Long Island to New York or Brooklyn and passing through boarded-up sections of East New York and Queens where black men warmed themselves over bonfires made from scraps of wood. I noticed during this part of the trip that my fellow commuters on the heated train did not look out of the window; they buried their heads in their newspapers or napped. This was long before the current-day epidemic of homelessness in America and before crime and drugs had spread to affluent neighborhoods. I remember feeling a sense of foreboding. Still, this was nothing at all compared to what I had seen in Rio de Janeiro or São Paulo or Recife or Natal, places I had visited during my dissertation research in Brazil. I never thought that Carolina Maria de Jesus's book represented any kind of experience shared by the poor in my own country.

As far as my memento from Rio was concerned, the boy's ink drawing, I had it framed; it hung in my office until it developed mold spots years later. When I later returned to Rio and again saw the sidewalk artist, he had grown up. He still squatted on the same spot outside the movie theater. Now, however, he drew florid, touristic drawings that lacked the simple beauty of his earlier works. My attempts to engage him in conversation failed. I knew little about favelas except that they filled the hills above Rio. Once when I was walking with a Peace Corps volunteer and another couple in Leblon, through the Praia do Pinto favela, we were held up and I was struck in the face with the butt of a revolver. The mugging made me jumpy during the remainder of my stay in Brazil. As a result, I walked away a bit faster when shabbily dressed black youths approached me on the street. My fascination about favelas, then, was rooted in my disappointment with Brazilians' lack of interest in improving conditions as well as in my personal fear of further violence.

When I started teaching in the autumn of 1966, I decided to add the recently published paperback diary, *Child of the Dark*, to the reading list of my introductory Latin American history course. I had read it while preparing my undergraduate classes, and some of my friends, newly appointed to other universities as Brazilian specialists, had commented on its suitability for classroom use. I was taken by how the diary described the misery of favela life and by the struggle of its author. I thought her message strangely contradictory: she hated her misery, she ached for a decent life for herself and her children, but at the same time she castigated her favela neighbors, harbored prejudices against northeasterners, and reviled fellow blacks. She was also patriotic when referring to Brazil's history and literature. She always recovered from her anger to display a weary but fanciful inclination: "when I have little to eat," she wrote, "I open the window of my hut and look at the heavens. . . . I'm too poor to go to plays," she added, "so God makes the stars perform in my honor." Leaves blowing softly in the wind she saw as applause for her "love for her country."[2]

The 1960s were an idealistic era and I wanted my students to read the testimony of a desperately-poor black woman who, I felt, was expressing the feelings of millions of heretofore silent Latin Americans. There was another, more practical reason for my repeated assignment of her diary to my students: the book was inexpensive and continually in print, unlike so many other books. Students were frequently moved by the book and intensely debated such questions as Carolina's acceptance of the system that so mistreated her, the reasons for the enormous gap between rich and poor in Latin America, and the fact that she was proud not only of being Brazilian but of being black.

Year after year her diary engaged the interest of students to whom I assigned it. I would ask them: Why was this women so docile? Their attempts to understand her would fill up the rest of the class hour. The simple language of *Child of the Dark* was easily understood by my students, even though most of them, including those of Hispanic background, might have been reading about the moon as far as their knowledge of Brazil was concerned. Carolina's words brought alive a slice of Latin American reality rarely acknowledged in traditional textbooks. During the early 1970s, with the help of Barbara Kantz, I produced several audio-visual projects for classroom use. I first used slides of scenes from Brazil and later transferred the slide show to videotape. Photocopying the book, I used scissors and paste to piece together a 20-minute abridged version of Carolina's text, focusing on the paradox between Carolina's descriptions of her terrible life and her lyrical expressions of thanks and satisfaction for having been born Brazilian.

The script emphasized her expressions of hope for her daughter, Vera Eunice, passages which I found especially touching. A visiting Brazilian student recorded a voice track and we fitted it to the visuals with Brazilian music. The production was amateurish and not copyrighted—the slides I used were mostly of Rio, not of São Paulo, where Carolina had lived— but my student audiences granted me poetic license and generally appreciated the production very much. Some Brazilians who saw the video, however, objected vehemently. Only now do I see that complaining about the use of "wrong" slides was a way for some of them to avoid discussing Carolina's narrative that portrayed a Brazil they refused to acknowledge.

The slide show was shown in many places, from middle-school classrooms in Suffolk County, Long Island, to the Latin American Studies Program at Yale and to the Columbia University Seminars on Latin America and on Brazil. It invariably provoked discussions about Brazil and about the burden of marginalized black women and about Carolina's seemingly contradictory personality. I chaired the Columbia Seminar on Brazil in those days, and showed the slide production (later made into a videotape) during one of the group's meetings. Shortly after one of the showings at Columbia, a free-lance film maker working under contract to the New York Public Television station, WPBS, contacted me. He asked if I could help him track down Carolina. Later I was told that the film maker abandoned his project because he received no cooperation from the Brazilian authorities whom he had contacted.

I happened to be in Rio in 1977 when Carolina Maria de Jesus's obituary appeared in the *Jornal do Brasil*. I was angered by what I considered to be the newspaper's insinuations blaming her for her death in poverty. She had not learned to take advantage of her celebrity status, it suggested, and had proved too stubborn and too demanding to improve herself. I was shaken by the obituary because nowhere did it acknowledge what I took to be her symbolic importance as the first voice in that nation's history to focus the attention of a mass audience on the pain and distress experienced by those at the bottom of society. The historical value of her book as well as her feisty insistence on maintaining her independence should have earned her recognition if not honor. Nevertheless, her death was not very much lamented in Brazil, and she was buried in a pauper's grave.

Time passed. The diary continued to be published in the United States—and in many countries in Europe—but when I travelled in Brazil I found that it had been out of print for years. Curious, I wrote to my friend José Carlos at USP, asking him if he knew anything further about Carolina Maria de Jesus. I also received assistance from the writer Nélida Piñón, my University of Miami colleague, who gently prodded the editors at Francisco Alves, Carolina's first Brazilian publisher, to show me copies of her book contracts. José Carlos's reaction was different: when I told him that I was writing an article about Carolina's story, and sent him a preliminary draft, he replied that Carolina was never very important and that Brazilian intellectuals had never expressed sympathy because she had been so conservative. She was certainly not a Brazilian Rigoberta Menchú, the Guatemalan Mayan woman who won the Nobel Prize for the harrowing memoir she dictated about her struggle for human rights.[3] Questions I addressed to other Brazilians about Carolina's importance as a writer and exemplary black woman produced discouraging results. Many, especially younger people, claimed never to have heard of her or, if they did, said that she had been a pest. Few responded when I asked why her books were no longer read in Brazil although the diary at the time of its publication in Brazil had sold more copies than any other book in that country's publishing history.

Benê (Benedito Fernando dos Santos) in his bar, Interlagos.
Photo by Robert M. Levine.

The always gracious and accommodating José Carlos Sebe Bom Meihy humored me by asking an undergraduate USP history student, Juliano Andrade Spyer, to help find copies of articles about Carolina in back issues of newspapers and research other materials about her life. Late in 1991, Juliano surprised me by writing that he had found the home of Carolina's daughter Vera and made arrangements to interview her. Vera, portrayed in Carolina's diary as a five-year-old carried on her mother's back when she scavenged for paper and for food, eventually married, became a teacher, and in 1994 was a part-time third-year night student at a small public college studying to be a translator of English materials.

I flew to São Paulo in late December 1992 to stay with José Carlos, his wife Alice and their boys, and to meet with José Carlos's oral history students. A group of us met with Vera Eunice de Jesus twice at a streetfront bar across from a bottled gas distributorship in the noisy working-class neighborhood of Interlagos; we also met once at her home. Benedito

Fernando dos Santos (Benê), the bar's proprietor, had played the part of Zé Carlos in the stage adaptation of Carolina's diary as a youthful child actor. He had met Zé Carlos again after Carolina died. Benê was then working as a military police *despachante* (expeditor). They became friends and, although the relationship remained one-sided because of Zé Carlos's alcoholism, Benê always stood ready to help. Benê eventually had earned a degree in law and knew both Vera and her surviving brother and acted as mediator after our first contacts. More than once Vera had called off the project because she feared that we were trying to take advantage of her by using her story for our profit. Benê calmly worked through the ramifications of the project and urged Vera to cooperate. At our second meeting at his bar we were joined by Zé Carlos, Vera, and her husband Paulo, and five of Carolina's grandchildren.

The encounter shook me. We drove in Juliano's broken-down Chevette through pounding traffic with temperatures in the nineties and noxious diesel fumes belching out of trucks and buses on all sides. We arrived at Benê's to find no one at the prearranged meeting place. We sat and rested and talked. About a half-hour later, a thin, grizzled man staggered by on the sidewalk behind the iron grating separating the bar from the street: drunk, he lurched forward, held onto the bars, and stared at us. I thought he was a beggar seeking a handout; it was Carolina's son, Zé Carlos. We asked him to come in. He excused himself to "take care of something" on the corner, where he had another drink of *cachaça* (cane liquor) at another bar. When he came back and sat down with us he was talkative in spite of his red and swollen eyes. He said that he had been sleeping in doorways but that he had gone to Vera's to take a shower and learned from her that we would be meeting to discuss our offer to turn over half of the royalties earned from our projected book to Vera's family (we had agreed that the student members of our team would receive the other half). He proceeded to discuss a wide range of topics that included the American rescue effort in Somalia (he approved), the incoming Clinton administration (he wasn't sure), the effects of Hurricane Andrew on Miami, and the numbers of Brazilians in the United States seeking a better life. He also discussed Vargas Llosa's fictionalized account of Euclydes da Cunha's *Os Sertões*, and, when told that my book about Canudos would be published in Brazil soon, he asked questions about it. I was astounded that this man, living in the streets and in such bad physical shape, was so

Vera, Paulo, their four children, and Zé Carlos's daughter (at far left).
Photo by Robert M. Levine.

remarkably well-versed. His mother, of course, had shown the same star-
tling awareness of the outside world. I had assumed that marginalized
people were ignorant and isolated. Zé Carlos showed me something else,
despite his drunkenness.

Things changed abruptly when Paulo, Vera's husband, drove up to the
bar in his battered old yellow Chevrolet station wagon and parked in
front. Zé Carlos sparred verbally with Paulo from the moment he entered. Zé Carlos moved his chair sideways to avoid eye contact with his
brother-in-law and made disparaging remarks about Vera (the "professor of the periphery" he shouted at one point), mocking the low status of
her job and the place where she was studying. Then Vera came in with
her four children and Zé Carlos's daughter, the youngest of the group,
whose head had been shaved because of lice. Vera's children were smiling
but Zé Carlos's daughter stared at the floor, conspicuously ill-at-ease. We
were the only occupants of the bar save for Benê, the proprietor, and a
few customers. Throughout the meeting Vera appeared almost overwhelmed by stress. At the same time she displayed an intense pride in

having made a better life for herself. In response to questions about her current university course of study to be a translator, she disparaged the institution for its poverty, but at the same time revealed great pride in acknowledging what she had achieved, and in the life she and her husband and her children were now able to live. Her family clearly had entered the salaried working class and were far removed from the destitution of her favela upbringing.

The personal exchange we witnessed between Zé Carlos and Vera was savage. When his daughter entered, eyes lowered, and sat down, he mockingly introduced her to the group as "my kid who has just been left back in school." "Your kid, right," said Vera; "none of my children have been left back." The discussion continued in this vein for a very, very long time. Frequently, Zé Carlos jumped up, grabbed his frayed plastic shopping bag filled with clothes and at least two hardcover books and started to leave the bar. Benê and the others brought him back. Vera remained equally angry, attacking him for forcing her to raise his daughter and for being a drunk. "I have no *din-din*," (*dinheiro*, money) he said more than once to Vera, "but I am not as stuck up as you are." He continued to pour down glasses of straight *cachaça* (cane alcohol). Finally, at the very moment when it seemed hopeless to continue, he grabbed the contract and, with a flourish, signed it, giving all of the 50 percent rights to his sister. He then made a dramatic exit and, for my benefit, said in English, "so long."

This may, of course, have been an act, since he knew that if Vera received the money she would not squander it, and that he would get some. He had amazed me with his flashes of knowledge about culture and about the world. On the way home, we all agreed that the transcript of his oral history was the most spontaneous and the most insightful recorded to date. I also will never forget the faces of Carolina's frightened grandchildren, one hoping to become a nurse, another a teacher, all polite and timid and nudging one another across the table during an ugly barrage of accusations and bitter recriminations.

Why had I been so drawn to Carolina's story? The book had become a part of me just as it had attained nearly iconographic status as a classic text used increasingly in the classroom in the United States. After teaching it to dozens of different groups of undergraduate and graduate students, I had memorized large segments of its text. I still found the book fresh in its expression of emotions, and I still puzzled at Carolina's refusal to condemn the system that had produced the misery in which she lived. I remained vexed at the contradiction of left-wing Brazilians espousing social revolution for Brazil while maintaining luxury residences and employing maids—often adolescents—paid pitiful wages for working six-and-a-half days a week. These were the conditions under which Carolina Maria de Jesus had worked as a domestic when she followed her dream of a better life in São Paulo. I was still astonished in the diary by Carolina's juxtaposition of moments of lyrical happiness with descriptions of favela noise and violence as she struggled to survive as a scavenger. Did Brazilians reject her because she spent precious food money to have a photograph taken so that she could get a voter ID card? Because she placed her family's welfare above feelings of solidarity with her fellow sufferers? Because she dreamed of eating decent food and living in a brick house rather than standing at the barricades? Because she and her three children would all sing together when they woke up in the morning?

We wrapped up the research portion of the study during my visit to São Paulo in July 1993. We learned from Vera that her brother Zé Carlos now had a new son, Jonas, around four months old. Vera showed us her mother's archive: in it we discovered the unpublished fragments that are translated for this book. We met with the student team and discussed finances. As noted earlier, José Carlos and I signed over our royalties from the book to Carolina's grandchildren. The USP students who had helped with the interviews now decided to donate their share to the Guarujá's Women's Association named after Carolina.

At dusk the next evening, friends drove me to the airport in rush-hour traffic. We drove through affluent Perdizes and streets of high-rise apartment complexes and single-family houses, each protected by armed guards. We passed a lit-up McDonald's crowded with affluent patrons (in Brazil, only the well-to-do eat in such places). Then we turned left at an intersection that led to the ugly Tietê Causeway and the road to the airport. To the left was a raised embankment on which stood three ragged young boys. The two older ones, perhaps seven or eight years old, stood together, back from the highway. Ten or fifteen feet away, at the curb, stood a child, no more than three or four. He was filthy and had a pacifier in his mouth. Pleading with his eyes, he lurched forward to touch the car window, begging. Caught up in the surging traffic behind him, the driver of our car reacted by stepping on the gas, forcing the child to lunge backward to avoid being hit. Crossing the intersection, we joined the kilometers-long line of trucks and busses and cars heading away from the city. The air was heavily polluted and rank with diesel fumes. We inched by in the heavy traffic. Now confined within concrete, the Tietê River in which Carolina Maria de Jesus had washed clothes was on our left. We passed the soccer stadium built on the site of the Canindé favela when it was torn down. Elsewhere, new favelas, even more precarious than Canindé had been, lined the causeway. Carolina's writings, in my mind, were more relevant than ever.

José Carlos Sebe Bom Meihy

I was seventeen when Carolina Maria de Jesus published her book. My view of my youth was necessarily colored by memories of later times, especially the 1970s, when the military government slowly restored some democratic institutions. Sometimes, when I think of terms like *golden years* used to describe the end of the 1950s, or the *rebellious years* of the second part of the 1960s, or even when I hear the phrase *years of iron* for the 1970s, I seek to fit these descriptions in a place between myth and fact. My memories of the 1950s are not so golden, nor are my recollections of the 1960s that of rebellion. More than repression, I recall the 1970s as times of seeking liberty and battling against the military dictatorship.

The poverty that I see in my memory, filtered through youthful experience, is striking. The interior city of Taubaté, São Paulo, where I grew up, was small; everyone knew everyone else. We knew the names of the poor people in our midst. Even their nicknames were not pejorative. Those were reserved for the drunks. Most of the poor were not alcoholics; we didn't confuse the two categories. I remember more the drunks from rich families, alienated people, people with amazing histories. The poor were simply *coitados*—hapless. In large and small cities alike the poor people foraged for paper and junk. Each had a marked-out territory. This system extended even to Canindé, Carolina's favela, as Maria Puerta tells us. The poor fit into our landscape naturally, as did the beggars. I remember women with handkerchiefs around their heads, old women with long, discolored dresses, men with sacks filled with junk on their shoulders, and children timidly asking for food. They were certainly dirty but this

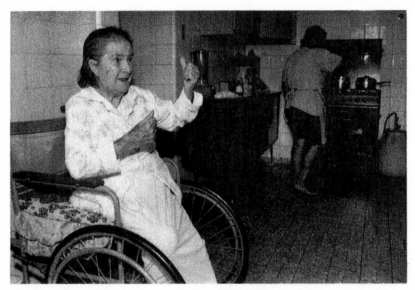

Maria Puerta at her home in São Paulo, 1993. Photo by Robert M. Levine.

image does not dominate my recollection. Nor do I remember being frightened that they might rob me, even if they were in need. It was gypsies, dressed in vivid-colored cloaks, who scared children. Seeing the poor on the street among us, in the markets, churches, outdoor squares, was different from seeing them in their own fetid habitats. So many things in our society—the schools, charity, social services, the government—served to segregate the rich and to domesticate the poor.

For the countries of Western Europe and especially for the United States, Carolina's story portrayed an unjust world reinforced by centuries of colonialism. For American liberals, Carolina's diary showed the corruption of the system. The book was also read avidly in socialist bloc countries. In the Eastern bloc as well as in Cuba, Carolina's book seemed to illustrate the contradictions of capitalism and its imminent exhaustion. The historical dynamic of each of these literary contexts: Brazilian, Latin American, European, North American; capitalist or socialist, suggests that there are many ways to read Carolina Maria de Jesus's words. Why did Carolina Maria de Jesus mean so many different things to so many different readers? How can we approach her work now, given how much has changed since she wrote her diaries? What frontiers did Carolina represent in her time, for Brazil, for Latin America, for Europe, for the rest of the world, for the United States?

I cannot escape my personal experiences as a member of the young urban generation that emerged in the euphoric years immediately before the armed forces' coup in 1964. In the early 1960s, I took a trip to the north and south of Brazil. What I saw shocked me; for someone from the State of São Paulo it was another country. In 1962 I went to Argentina and in the following year to Europe. After the 1964 military coup, I went as an exchange student to the United States. There I constantly thought of my own country from the perspective of what I was seeing at a distance. Like many of the middle-class youths who left Brazil to travel, I returned with a different way of seeing the transition between old and new in Brazil.

On the other hand, the experience of living with a family in the state of Georgia after attending a small high school in the interior of Pennsylvania punctured the idyllic view of life in the United States I had absorbed through the propaganda about the American way of life before my departure from Brazil. I was one of those students who were critical of the U.S. as the leader of the capitalist world. Yet I also wanted to take advantage of the benefits offered by North American consumerism. Studying in the United States during the 1960s, however, gave me a different picture of that country. I remember the images of the 1963 Civil Rights march on Washington led by Martin Luther King Jr. I also opposed the Vietnam War, and especially remember reading years later an interview with Cassius Clay (Muhammad Ali) explaining the abuses suffered by blacks drafted for that war. To be in the midst of black southerners after the passage of the Civil Rights Act in August 1964 marked me and permitted me to observe the differences in race relations in the two countries. Later on I watched with curiosity as the Black Panthers exploded the argument that Brazilian and American blacks tended to act in the same way. I remember vividly the references to Brazil by people I met when I arrived in the United States: mostly about the Amazon, samba, soccer, but little else. Carmen Miranda, the singer whose hats filled with tropical fruits and feathers enchanted Hollywood, was about the only Brazilian person most people knew about. It was irritating to hear that Buenos Aires was Brazil's capital, and no less annoying to hear the perception—shared by some Brazilians, of course—that Brazil was unsuited for democracy: that a military government was something to be expected. Many people did know about Carolina Maria de Jesus; they identified her name with Brazil.

I had read the Brazilian edition of *Child of the Dark* shortly after it was published. With youthful eyes I paid attention, as did many Brazilians, to the woman denouncing the conditions and insidious effects of favela life. I watched the rise of this "Black Cinderella." I confess that some aspects of the book disconcerted me and led me to doubt that she could be considered either a rebel or even a revolutionary. Her loyalty to Adhemar de Barros (mayor of the city of São Paulo and later governor) bothered me, because of the corruption that surrounded him. I also came to see Audálio Dantas's hand and wondered about how much of the book had been his. In the end, I asked myself, could Carolina have existed without Audálio? All of the events—the newspaper series, the book, the magazine coverage, Carolina's public appearance, seemed part of an interconnected web.

Living as an exchange student within the black student milieu in Georgia permitted me to gain better insight into the mechanics of race relations in the American South. I reconsidered the conservative Brazilian writer Monteiro Lobato's arguments about the American race issue, especially his treatment of the subject in his book, *The Negro President*, that proposed a tragic end for American blacks and that colored my analysis of the speeches of Malcolm X, who in fact attracted me more than his peaceful rival, Martin Luther King. These were the most agitated years of the American Civil Rights movement. They affected me profoundly. Leaving the mostly rural Paraíba Valley, a place so quiet and domesticated, exposed to a world far more dynamic and reform-minded, I was caught in the dilemma of the race issue in two cultures. Also, I thought about the differences between the two countries. What a contrast there was between Carolina Maria de Jesus and American black-power activists! It occurred to me to ask why Carolina touched so many North Americans, and why hadn't the culture and outlook of American blacks reached us in Brazil? In any case, the experience permitted me to see beyond the stereotype that the United States was simply a "racist" country. While still in the American South I began to read the folklorist and sociologist Gilberto Freyre's books and think about how his writings had influenced the ways Brazilians thought about race. I reread *Tempo de Aprendiz*, about Freyre's travels in the United States between 1918 and 1926. Did we really have a "racial democracy," as he argued? Not only did I admire the American black-power movement, but I began to question the situation at home and the differences in the ways Americans and Brazilians see racial issues. In Brazil, we deal (or fail to deal) with race on the basis of individuals. In the United States, society is divided into all-encompassing groups (blacks, whites, Hispanics, Asians), and race becomes a matter for governments and laws.

My reading of Carolina Maria de Jesus's diary, then, was different from that of Americans. They saw it as protest literature; I did not. I paid attention to Carolina's animosity towards northeasterners, to her romantic liaisons, always with white men, as characteristic of the way she saw the world. I examined the way she talked about the favela, and measured whether she was more concerned about race than about poverty. She never took part in community action within the favela; she wrote to escape. Her life stands apart. Given that in Brazil the condition of being black carries with it the condition of being miserable, before protesting against poverty, one must consider the color question as well. After all, Carolina, writing for whites, represents the traditional defensiveness of Brazilian black literature. She does not dwell on the question of racial identity. Rather, she sought to live in peace in a better world, the world of whites. Considering Carolina's work as black writing raised questions about the limits of social acceptance open to blacks in Brazil. If traditionally blacks have been able to ascend the Brazilian social ladder in the artistic or entertainment field (for all practical purposes, either through music or soccer), Carolina followed a different path from the one blazed by blacks like Pelé who managed to achieve success as performers. Her path was literary. She wrote the book that sold more copies than any other in our history.

I returned from the United States and completed my graduate studies. I became a university professor and working historian. It so happened that in 1978 I was asked to be the academic mentor and coordinator at my university for a program involving visiting undergraduates from universities in the United States. The selection process required that prospective participants write a short essay about their understanding of Brazilian culture. Invariably they wrote something about Carolina's diary. If on one hand I was unhappy about this, on the other I thought it important that the students learn in person that Carolina, after becoming a national celebrity, had ended up largely forgotten just as the world she described changed beyond recognition.

My contact with many of the foreign graduate students and professors specializing in Brazilian history and culture who kept arriving in Brazil increased my indignation at the ways Brazil was explained elsewhere, especially in the United States. The frequency with which *Child of the Dark* appeared in course reading lists on Brazil was astonishing. I heard many different reasons for this, but the one told to me most frequently was simply that this was one of only a very small number of books available about "our urban reality" narrated by someone inside, from within the domain of misery represented by favela life. In truth, save for Jorge Amado's novels, some pieces by Machado de Assis, and more recently Clarice Lispector, there was virtually nothing in English written by Brazilians that could be adopted by someone developing a syllabus about Brazil. I add to this list the history of the Republic by José Maria Bello and João Cruz Costa's short essay on philosophy. The rest of the books available seemed all to have been written by foreign Brazilianists.

It is evident that Carolina was important for Brazil. Her success cannot merely be explained as the work or journalists or editors. While Carolina rejected and fled favela life, she was also marked by it. Her achievement in getting out, in joining (at least for a while) the world of affluent whites, is something that has to be recognized as an unprecedented achievement. Being black in a world of whites, being a woman in a world dominated by men, finding it impossible to manage her money when her pot of gold appeared, if briefly, at the end of her rainbow, was very difficult for her. Highs and lows buffeted her, and she died poor and forgotten. The stress of her difficult life left visible effects on her children, Vera and Zé Carlos. One hopes that her grandchildren will grow up with a greater degree of equilibrium, that they will free themselves of the encumbrances of their grandmother's memory while at the same time cherishing her accomplishments.

The fact that Carolina achieved her fame during the early 1960s is critically important. These years were not only years of hope for Brazil, but they represented a transitory period between the old era of Getúlio Vargas and the post-1964 years of the military dictatorship. Carolina, who came to maturity during the Vargas years, in many ways was a model Vargas citizen. She was sober, she possessed an unbending work effort, and more than anything else she wanted to be a good mother for her children. These traits received less emphasis during the late 1950s and early 1960s, when planners turned to developmentalist solutions on a massive, national scale. The continued popularity of *Child of the Dark* in United States academic circles as a statement about Brazilian poverty perplexes me, because it suggests that Brazilianists there do not understand how dated it is. Carolina could not have survived in São Paulo favela today. The city has become so transformed by its industrial boom that a sole migrant lacking the support network of an extended family would be overwhelmed and entrapped. Nor would a journalist be likely to do with a new Carolina what Dantas did. There is no more local news; journalism has become internationalized.

2
From the Favela to the Moon

Carolina Maria de Jesus was born in 1914 in the town of Sacramento, located on a high plateau in the backlands "Triangle" of the State of Minas Gerais near the São Paulo border. Two-thirds of the residents were illiterate. The poorest were blacks; coffee-complexioned, mixed-race *mulatos* also lived austerely but enjoyed higher status (and less menial jobs). Despite a reasonable amount of economic activity at the turn of the century, including cheese manufacturing, coffee production, and rice and bean agriculture, the area had steadily declined in importance in the ensuing decades and its population dwindled. During the 1920s, when Carolina was growing up, it had ten unpaved streets and almost no public services. In 1950, when Carolina's relatives still lived there and she occasionally visited, there were fewer than 4,000 inhabitants, more women than men.[1] Carolina descended from slaves and was illegitimate.[2] Her maternal grandfather, Benedito José da Silva, was highly regarded among the town's blacks for his wisdom and love for learning although he never attended school. He fathered eight children. His oldest daughter was Maria Carolina, the author's mother. Carolina later was given her mother's name, with *Carolina* and *Maria* placed in reverse order. Her father was an itinerant musician from the Minas Gerais town of Araxá, João Cândido Veloso. He wandered from one small café to another serenading patrons for tips. A married man and alcoholic, he broke off with Carolina's mother, Maria Carolina, forcing her to take the only jobs open to her in the town, cleaning house for prostitutes. During all of her childhood, Carolina and

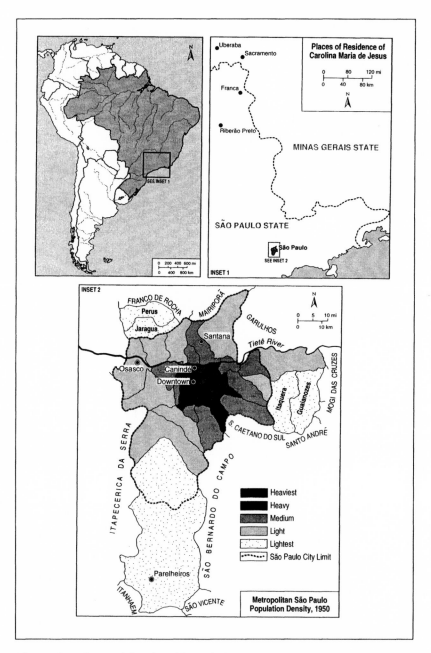

Places of residence of Carolina Maria de Jesus.

her family were treated as pariahs in the town, even though her grandfather held the respect of the entire community. Carolina, as a female child with an aggressive personality, bore the brunt of the ostracism more than anyone else in her family.

Carolina's mother later lived for a time with a man whom Carolina called her stepfather, but the liaison was never legitimized by marriage, an act considered mandatory in a region so traditional that teachers addressed their eight-year old pupils by the formal "a Senhora" (ma'am). Putting a good face on her early life, Carolina as an adult described her father to her own daughter Vera as a "bohemian." He was also, in his granddaughter's words, so black that his skin seemed blue. Brazilians during the 1920s—just as now—rendered very close attention to a person's skin color. In almost all cases, the darker one's complexion, the more difficult it was to advance in society. Being illegitimate *and* a poor black female was an even greater obstacle, especially in the small rural towns of Minas Gerais. Growing up as an object of scorn and racial discrimination, Carolina's difficult early years left scars. She developed traits of self-pity and self-hatred, probably the result of the ugly prejudice levelled against her. She became ambivalent about her blackness, as well. Although her autobiographical writings are filled with statements of pride about having been born black, all throughout her life she was attracted to white men, and she detested blacks from her social class.

Affluent Brazilians during the early twentieth century were enamored of progress. Elites worked to give their towns and cities the appearance of being modern, despite the survival of a rigid social system that effectively kept the poor—especially those with dark skin—in their place. Sacramento received electric street lighting in 1910, a very early date for a place so remote. That same year the mayor had a trolley line installed connecting Sacramento with Cipó more than a dozen kilometers to the south where passengers could connect with a railroad line travelling to the city of Franca across the border and then on to the booming metropolis of São Paulo.[3] While the tiny local upper class basked in its own self-importance, life in Sacramento for blacks was so crude that they had to produce nearly everything they used, even soap. They bartered only for cloth, kerosene, and salt.

Bitita, as Carolina was nicknamed, was sent to school at the age of seven. She was fortunate to have been able to do so, the result of the personal philanthropy of Maria Leite, a landowner's wife from the countryside near of Sacramento. She was a member of the spiritist cult named for the French medium Alain Kardec; in an act highly unusual for the time, she paid the tuition and school expenses of Carolina and several poor black children to the sect-run school as personal penance for her ancestors having owned slaves.[4] Initially, Bitita was not a willing student—she did not know how to act around whites, even when they were kind to her—and her mother had to spank her practically every day to make her attend. Later, she came to love school and valued it desperately for her own children.

Carolina's later description of her student days is telling. At first her mother did not want to accept Maria Leite's charity, but Mrs. Leite, who visited Sacramento to check up on the school, prevailed. Carolina remarked later that she thought that her benefactor was named "Leite" [milk] because of her white skin. Mrs. Leite used to touch the heads of the black children and say that they reminded her of black pepper. To motivate them, she told the children that she liked black people and that she wished that she had been born black too. She said that if she were younger she would establish her own schools to help further. She asked the children to read to her and gave gifts of money to the ones who performed well. The contrast between Mrs. Leite's open-mindedness and her own mother's passivity astounded Carolina, although she always referred to her mother as "blessed." "My mother was timid," she wrote later. "She said that blacks should obey whites."

In fact, Carolina's initial attendance at school resulted more from her mother's desire to satisfy Mrs. Leite than from any maternal interest in education. Her mother accepted her fate as an outcast. She told Carolina that "whites were the true masters of the world." Carolina said she always felt humiliated when her mother said "yes, ma'am" and "yes, sir" when addressing whites. This defiance of the society's racial conventions was an early mark of the personality trait that in later years would give Carolina the reputation of a disrespectful troublemaker. As a child, Carolina often experienced color prejudice and expressions of racial attitudes that caused her great pain. Sometimes mulatos and other blacks cursed her because she was not only black but illegitimate and terribly poor. When white girls picked on her they called her "stinky nigger" and insulted her frizzy black hair. Black youngsters in Sacramento were commonly called "children of monkeys." Some white schoolmates even incited Carolina to throw rocks at other blacks. Later in her life, in her autobiographical writings, Carolina professed that some of her lighter-skinned relatives (*mulatos*, because one of their parents was light complexioned) spurned her when she was growing up. A cousin, Adam Nunes (who was a *mulato*), mocked her for having "airs" because she used big words, brushed her teeth, and bathed—all things, he said, that proved she was trying to imitate white people. Her uncle Joaquim, a black man who lived with Carolina's godmother, a sickly white woman, was taunted by both blacks and whites ("sugar with coffee, coffee with milk, a mosquito in milk"). This hapless woman had formerly been married to a black named Alcides who had abandoned her, possibly because she was unable to bear children. She was as thin as a rail. Ultimately, her uncle left her behind in Sacramento, unable to find work and to escape the beatings by policemen because he had a white wife. Carolina was terrified of the human skeletons displayed on the walls of the schoolhouse. At seven, Carolina was unusually dependent. She still was being nursed by her mother when she entered school, but her teacher shamed her into stopping. Angry with the girl for a number of reasons, the teacher slapped her on the legs with a ruler and refused to let her go home to be nursed. Carolina's mother, however, expressed delight at what the teacher had done because it freed her from the need to nurse. Hurt by her mother's attitude and by the humiliation she felt, Carolina performed badly in school at first. Once, when she had displayed a lack of interest, her teacher drew a picture of a man holding a trident with a child skewered on it on the blackboard. She then warned Carolina in front of the class that this man was the school inspector and that at the end of the year he would do this to children who had not learned to read and write. Carolina was terrified by the image and resolved to change her ways. Because she was exceptionally bright, the opportunity to use her mind and to be rewarded for it was exhilarating for her. Soon she became an excellent student, studying assiduously and learning to read within three months, astonishing her mother by reading shop signs as they walked along the street. She quickly read everything she could get her hands on. The teacher lent her books, mostly religious ones, including the New Testament and a life of St. Theresa.

During her two years of primary school, Carolina not only learned to write but developed clear, legible penmanship.

Until she was a teenager, Carolina lived with her younger brother, her mother, and her mother's common law husband. Because of their poverty, the family wore sandals, not shoes, and their house had a roof made of thatch. Two years after she entered school, when she was nine, her stepfather, as she called him, decided to find work as a sharecropper in the interior. He found a job on a *fazenda* (farmstead) at Lageado, near Uberaba, a fairly large city on the Minas Gerais side of the border with the State of São Paulo. Carolina cried when she had to leave school after only two years. After packing her books she rode with her family to Lageado on a truck driven by a friend—her first truck ride in her life. Books became her solace and her only refuge in the countryside. Her stepfather labored at planting and harvesting rice, beans, corn, and sugar cane, all for the landowner. On a smaller, unused plot he was permitted to sow squash, okra, and fava beans for the family's own use. Carolina's mother was made to work in the landowner's house without wages. Carolina's first days in the country were spent, in her words, crying. Black, illegitimate, miserably poor, ostracized, Carolina continued reading and attempting to learn about the world. Many adults with whom she came into contact were startled by her. Once in Sacramento her mother set out to beat her because a teacher, Eurípedes Barsanulfo, referred to her daughter as a "poetess." The mother, consulting with her neighbors, figured out that this must mean some kind of evil. Eventually, Carolina succumbed to the psychological pressures of having to cope with gross ignorance. Even the thrill of her school setting in Sacramento, where, unlike most rural poor youngsters, she had been encouraged to excel, was quickly extinguished by the realities of rural life where children were not extended such luxuries. She grew up with no friends, either in Sacramento or in the countryside. Soon after her family arrived in Lageado, she was told that she too had to labor at chores all day in the landowner's house for no wages. This was the custom in rural areas, but Carolina, not yet ten years old, did not expect to be made to work.

The work environment in Lageado was unusually stressful for Carolina and her family. The landowner and his wife were cousins and both their two children had been born with genetic defects. The daughter was a deaf mute unable to walk, perhaps owing to emotional or psychological disturbances. She ate her food from the floor, sometimes mixed with her own feces. The son was also retarded and, although he had spent some years at a special school in Rio de Janeiro, had never progressed very much. The landowner's dream, Carolina said, was to have a son with "Doctor" before his name. These children, she reasoned, were the man's payment for having married for money. "I came to the conclusion," she wrote, "that it was God's design to balance the inequities in each one's life." Carolina describes their first meeting: "(W)hen my turn came the madam looked me over as if I were an object being appraised for sale. She said that I must be a clever black girl because I was slim with fine bones, she was reacting with envy because my mother had a perfect daughter. There was so much envy when they spoke I could read it in her face." Carolina later recollected (or perhaps she imagined) that D. Maria Cândida then made a promise: "You know, Carolina, you have to work for me, and when I go to Uberaba, I'll bring you a new dress, and a medicine to make you turn white, and another medicine to straighten your hair. Then I'll get a doctor to make your nose narrower." Carolina recalls thinking: "Then these people here used to be blacks. They don't like blacks, so they change blacks into whites. . . . And when I turn white, with my hair straightened and an aquiline nose, I want to go to Sacramento for my relatives to see me."

She was disappointed, of course: "I worked for D. Maria Cândida for six months. I awoke at five in the morning, washed my face in a hurry because I tried always to arrive on time so my mistress wouldn't be angry at me. I rejoiced when she told me one day that she was going to Uberaba. I awaited her return with great anxiety. She stayed away two days. When she returned, she found me waiting on the porch. I was disappointed, however: she brought no packages. She'd fooled me. I thought about the six months work I had done for her without receiving a cent. I started to sob. My mother told me that blacks should not complain. I looked at my black hands and my broad nose and kinky hair and decided to remain the way I was born. I asked nothing of D. Maria Cândida. She had used a trick to deceive me. I couldn't curse her because she had given us permission to plant on her land. Plagues, as a result, had come down on her. I understood that she was paying through her idiot children."

On the other hand, Bitita envied the children of the Italian agricultural colonists brought in to sharecrop nearby, especially their optimism about the future. These immigrants told their children: "Three years from now we'll be rich. And you can study to be doctors." The children toiled in the fields singing Verdi arias, which the Brazilian children learned as well. Many European immigrants settled in rural southern and southcentral Brazil, and they are usually portrayed as keeping their distance from native-born rural workers, who typically were dark-skinned like Carolina and her family. It is characteristic of Carolina's personality that even as a deprived child she saw the best in people and never resented their better fortunes. She was intimidated, nonetheless, by contacts with those more powerful than her. When she and her mother traveled on foot to Uberaba to sell the food they had grown, they were terrified of the soldiers of the Fourth Minas State Battalion stationed in the city. With the money they made, they bought cloth, kerosene, salt, and thread; they journeyed back to Lageado in silence.

Despite being required to work and her initial anger at having to leave school, it was in Lageado that Carolina formed the memories that in later years—when things were much worse for her—would be expressed as a longing, even a love, for rural life. Her family acquired chickens and pigs and regularly consumed milk, butter, and cheese. "I looked around," she wrote in her memoirs. "Just trees and the blue sky with the sun like a tepid disk . . . . I began to appreciate the countryside's silence," she concluded. She listened to nature's sounds while she toiled with a hoe in the fields, and on Sunday, when she did not have to work outside, she lay in bed listening to the birds "with the impression that they were performing for me."[5] Again, however, her family was forced to relocate. Although Carolina cherished the quiet of the countryside and its abundance of food, after four years the sharecropping arrangement failed and her stepfather found himself in debt. The family moved back to Sacramento where they were still outcasts, and they found life no easier than before. Carolina recalled later:

> it was horrible to live among people who didn't respect us. Every day there were fights that attracted the police and ended in beatings. I missed the rural zone so much. I remembered when my mother used to roast manioc and make bread. My hands had become calloused, but my days were tranquil and I was not afraid of what the next day would bring. I was calm because I lived amidst plenty. I forgot about suffering. My mother watched over my life. I believed

in books as if they were my friends. Now the daily routine made me angry. People went in and out of my house., my cousins, and other intruders. On Saturdays everything was crazy in the house. . . the clothes iron passing from hand to hand. Everyone getting ready to go to a dance, the only distraction in the life of the poor.

One day a black labor recruiter came to Sacramento looking for agricultural workers to go to the *fazenda* Santa Cruz on the São Paulo side of the state line. The *fazenda* overseer, a Spaniard known as Loló was willing to employ Carolina's family harvesting coffee beans, but he denied permission to plant garden crops and paid only in vouchers redeemable at the local store. One by one the workers ran away: Carolina's stepfather first, then another sharecropper and his family, then Carolina's mother with Carolina and her brother. As a result, they were poorer than before. They had earned nothing and had been forced to leave their meager personal possessions behind. In disappointment, they returned once again to a life of poverty in Sacramento.

Still, these daunting events did not crush Carolina's spirit. She was an astute observer of the life around her. She knew that her family was achingly poor but she was always compassionate toward others. On some occasions she watched as victims of the northeastern droughts trekked through Sacramento mostly en route to the city of São Paulo. These wretched migrants carried their household possessions on their backs and appeared to Carolina to be human skeletons, dead on the inside. Most of them were *caboclos*, dark-complexioned mixed-race descendants of African slaves, Portuguese colonizers, and native Brazilians. Carolina noted that they were scorned not only by well-to-do townspeople but by her black neighbors as well. Sacramento's blacks lived in penury, but at least they had a place to call their home. The migrants had been driven by drought and forced to wander from the lands on which their families had lived for generations. Permanence, even in a place as miserable as Sacramento, afforded dignity to poor rural Brazilian men and women.

Still, life for destitute blacks in the small towns and cities of the interior was cruel and frequently violent. Once Carolina's mother attempted to stop a man from savagely beating his wife in public, the man grabbed her as well, throwing her down and stepping on her face. When the police arrived they arrested both the abuser and Carolina's mother. "[The police] were stupid men," Carolina later wrote in her memoirs, "barely literate. The ones who could spell the word *babá* (nursemaid) were promoted. . . . In those days poor people were always being arrested," she said. "Rich people were immune, protected by their safe-conduct passes, their writs of habeas corpus, and their money."[6] Once she saw a soldier slay a black man: "He was from the country, and he started to run away, frightened. The policeman shot him . . . . The policeman who fired the fatal shot wisecracked: 'What good aim I have. I'll get a medal for marksmanship.'" He prodded the body with his foot and said "he must be from Bahia [a reference to the place from which many migrants had come]." Carolina asked the policeman if the man had a mother. She remarked: "Who will cry for his death? He didn't fight, he didn't insult anyone. There were no reasons to kill him. He was carrying a package that was coming open. He came to the city to buy medicine. He was married with two children. When the police chief arrived he looked at the body and ordered it buried." No one knew the man's full name.

Carolina later told her daughter Vera that when she was an adolescent local families forbade their sons to talk with her. She also claimed that she was prohibited from entering the local Catholic church because her mother had raised two illegitimate children. Still, even though she was not allowed to attend mass and almost certainly never took communion, she considered herself to be a devout Catholic, the religion of most Brazilians. This was consistent with her developing personality, perhaps in compensation for the constant ostracism she faced. Instead, she constructed a personal world of her own making. All through her life she displayed a fierce sense of integrity. She learned from her mother and grandfather to have an intense work ethic and she disparaged people she thought lazy. She was constantly tormented and frustrated over the way blacks were treated in Brazil. Her difficult life marked her. Alone as a child because so many people rejected her, later in her life she erected a wall around herself by adopting behavior traits considered unseemly for a woman, including steadfastly refusing to be controlled by others, especially men. No saint, she came to hold many of the same stereotypical attitudes against poor blacks that others hurled at her. But she hated the effects of prejudice in society, and frequently yearned for the day when her fellow citizens would remember the Golden Law [the 1888 act that freed the slaves] and make it possible for blacks to be considered equals to other Brazilians.

In 1937 when Carolina was fourteen, her grandfather, whom she adored, became gravely ill. He was so forceful a personality that although he was black and poor, three rich white citizens of Sacramento "who read the newspaper *O Estado de São Paulo* and who knew what was going on in the world" visited her grandfather's house as he lay ill. Recalling the death watch in her memoirs, Carolina pointed out sarcastically that "the rich visited him because they understood him; the poor came out of curiosity." Blacks, she said, called him the "African Socrates." When Carolina asked her mother what the name Socrates meant, her mother, who probably did not know, scolded her and called her a vagabond. Later in life, when she learned who Socrates was, she frequently lamented that her grandfather had been denied formal education because of racial discrimination.

In spite of her constant battle with adversity, Carolina showed her mettle. Miraculously, she developed such positive self-esteem that her attitude angered many who expected her to behave as meekly as other poor black women. Her relations with persons in authority were influenced by her demand that she be treated with dignity. Some powerful individuals respected her for her plucky disposition but, more commonly, her assertiveness got her into trouble. Both in Sacramento and later in São Paulo, Brazil's leading metropolis, few people expected a woman from her servile background to read books, to have opinions, or to stand up for herself. In her memoirs she related one such example from her teenage years in the interior:

> One day, walking through the streets, I found a lime on a tree. I was happy because it is nice to get presents. I went to give it to my mother, but Humberto Brand came up to me and took away my lime. He was white and had served in the army. . . . To impress us, sometimes he wore a green uniform and terrorized the poor girls by grabbing their breasts. When the poor girls saw him they covered their breasts with their hands and ran away. . . . When I saw him, I yelled at him: 'Give me my lime! Give me my lime!' Everyone was afraid of him because he was the son of the judge. . . . When I passed by the front of his house he accosted me. 'Look at your limes, you black vagabond,' he said. He threw several limes at my face and legs. My nose began to bleed. He laughed. I cursed him: 'Dog . . . common person. No one likes you here. Get out of here. You are

dirty. You are white outside only. You bother poor girls. You don't grab the breasts of rich girls. People like you only respect money. You'll always be rotten. . . .' Dr. Brand [the Judge] interrupted: 'Don't you have manners?' 'I have,' I said; it is your son who doesn't. 'Shut your mouth! I can have you arrested.' I responded: 'So your son can do these awful things to me like he does with the other girls?' 'It's better to go to hell than to go to your house.'[7]

When Carolina was sixteen her mother moved to Franca, closer to the capital city of São Paulo but still 398 kilometers away. There mother and daughter worked together as domestic servants under very harsh conditions. Carolina found it more and more difficult to find work, even as a maid. Carolina's description of what happened when she sought treatment for a chronic infection on her legs at the charity hospital in Riberão Preto, a city in the interior of São Paulo, reveals the pathetic condition she found herself in and the hostility of the *mulato* branch of her family who lived there. It also illustrates the remarkable extent to which she would fight to survive. She retold the story, with its striking Cinderella metaphor, forty years later.

Carolina's mother had given her what little money she had: barely enough for train fare. Carolina arrived in Riberão Preto at dusk on Friday evening and paid the remainder of her money to the station porter to let her sleep at the depot and wake her at 6:00 A.M. Unless she knew that she'd be awakened, she thought, she'd be too worried to doze. In the morning, shaking with anxiety, she walked up the main avenue to the charity hospital and asked for an appointment to have her festering legs examined. A nurse applied a salve to her legs and told her to come back in three days. Carolina had no more money but was too frightened to protest. Instead, she decided to seek out her Aunt Ana, who lived in a neighborhood called Vila Tibério. It took her all day to find the house. When she arrived, at 6:00 P.M., her aunt's family was having dinner. Carolina greeted her aunt at the door, saying "Bless you, Aunt Ana," but the woman said nothing. Carolina's feet were badly swollen and she was hungry so she pushed her way through the door. Her cousins were *mulatos*, and although they were working-class people, they seemed wealthy by Carolina's standards. Because of her mother's low status among her relatives, however, and because Carolina was black, they showered her with contempt. Carolina's memoirs describe the scene: Aunt Ana told me: "You surely have eaten." "No, ma'am," I replied. She gave me a furious look. She put down a small serving of beans and rice, and said: "I'm not interested in having mouths visit me. Visits of arms, yes. How did you find my house?" "A woman told me." "My aunt became furious, cursing: 'Ah! A disgraceful, infamous woman . . . She can go to hell.'"

Carolina ate what she was served but remained hungry. Her cousins then began to get dressed for a dance that the family was going to attend, at a rented ballroom. They decided that she should accompany them because, as one said, they couldn't leave her in the house because she might be a thief. She had nothing beside the clothing she was wearing, of course, so she went in the same tattered dress she had worn on the trip from Sacramento. At the dance, her cousin Marcelina, who was closest to her in age and engaged to a youth named Octávio, behaved like a social butterfly, mingling with everyone. Carolina was impressed at the comportment of the guests and the way they dressed. The men wore fine suits. Watching her cousins dance, she said, she thought that they were from the other side of the world. At midnight, the dance organizers raffled off a roast chicken. Carolina, faint with hunger, felt tempted to steal it and run away.

By this time in Carolina's life she had become adept at watching things from the sidelines, since she was excluded from so much. She absorbed what she saw vicariously and analyzed its meaning. This had a calming effect on her; she realized that being petulant wouldn't help. She rationalized her social position and treatment. *Mulatos* were always spiteful to her, she remembered: in a world dominated by whites, *mulatos* acted as if they were better than blacks. She also felt sorry for herself. She was diseased, she told herself, and sick people need to be quarantined. She noticed that her aunt was sitting next to an "old" woman, more than fifty years of age. The woman asked Ana who the girl with her was. Ana looked her niece over minutely and responded: "She's a beggar who comes from time to time to my house to ask for handouts." "How charitable you are," the woman replied. To mark the end of the dance, the organizers announced that everyone present should join in a quadrille. Even Carolina was asked to join. Her legs were swollen and so heavy they felt made of lead. Pleased at being asked, she accepted. She felt like a badly dressed fairy tale character. She implored God to make the quadrille finish because she felt so much pain in her infected legs. When they arrived home her aunt gave her a rug on which to lay down on the cement floor. It was too dusty to sleep on, so she spent the night in a chair too hungry to sleep properly. In the middle of the night her cousin José Marcelino, a train engineer on the line to Sertãozinho, entered the kitchen, heated coffee, drank it, and left for work without offering any to her.

At daybreak Carolina went outside to warm in the sun. No one offered her any breakfast and someone complained about having had to pay for Carolina's admission ticket to the dance. She was told to stay in the yard out of the house. At mid-day her aunt gave her two spoons of rice and two of beans while complaining that she was a burden. "Why don't you beg?," she said. "Go to the city. I'm sick of you being here in my house. I left Sacramento so I wouldn't have to be mixed up with your family. . . ." Carolina then walked out. She found the house of another *mulata* relative, Barbara, who lived nearby. But when Barbara saw her at the door, she slammed it in her face. She returned to Ana's house and dozed in the yard. When she awoke, they had already eaten dinner. Still dirty from her trip, with the daytime temperatures rising to more than 90°, she was not permitted to bathe. During her three days at her aunt's she was only fed twice. When she left the house on the third day to go to her hospital appointment, she had to beg for bread along the way, lest she collapse.

When Carolina arrived at the hospital—the Santa Casa de Misericordia—she was terrified that she would be turned away because she stank after five hot days in the same unwashed clothes. She was afraid that she would never recover, that she would have to live in the streets already crowded with disfigured beggars. The nuns who received her, however, were kind. She was invited in graciously and offered a bath. When they gave her a towel to dry herself and a robe and night dress to wear, she cried with relief and gratitude. She was fed and put to bed and slept through the day and night. When she awoke, at 5:00 A.M., she heard birds chirping. Employing the recuperative powers that would serve her well throughout her life, she blessed the day. Weeks passed and the sores on her legs improved, although they did not completely heal. Now another side of her personality asserted itself. She was so accustomed to being rejected that she turned against people who helped her. Although the nuns implored her to stay for additional treatment, Carolina insisted on returning to Sacramento. Because she had no money she was forced to sleep on the side of the road while she walked the entire way back. By some miracle, in the small town of Salles Oliveira she saw a sign in a window advertising for a servant and got the job. For cleaning, waxing, washing, and cooking, she earned a pittance, but Carolina was delighted. Her employer was a taxi driver and his wife a seamstress. The job ended after two weeks but her employers helped her find another position working for two physicians, a husband and wife. She was made to feel comfortable. Dr. Manso praised her handwriting and complemented her on her teeth, which he called "snow-white." He also treated her legs. Carolina found a dictionary (she had never seen one) and used it to find out what "snow white" meant. Dra. Mietta brought her three dresses. After several weeks, however, Carolina's generous employers told her that they were relocating to Rio de Janeiro. Her employment ended, but she kept the dictionary and some books that had been given to her.

In Sacramento her mother scolded her for returning, since having another mouth to feed was a difficult burden. Spurned even by her immediate family, Carolina found refuge more than ever in books, including a copy of Camões's epic saga, *The Lusiaids*, the most famous classic in the Portuguese language. She sat in the shade under a tree and read for hours, but even this did not bring her peace. People walking by saw the young black woman reading her thick books and called her a witch. Once some youths reported her for sorcery to the police sergeant. Even though he was her cousin Leonor's godfather, he ordered his soldiers to arrest Carolina. Her mother protested when the police came for Carolina and she was arrested for interfering. The two women were kept in jail for five days without being fed and were frequently beaten with rubber truncheons. A relative brought them some meat with manioc flour or they might have died. When they were finally released, Carolina's mother's arm was so bruised from her injuries that she could not take in laundry, her usual way of earning money. The mother was fined 20 milréis—half a month's wages in Sacramento—by the jailer.

During the mid-1930s her mother's health failed, and she was abandoned by her lover, the man Carolina's refers to as her step-father. Her mother's inability to work made Carolina's burden even greater. Eventually they moved to Riberão Preto so that Carolina could find work as a domestic. In difficult circumstances, Carolina cared for her mother until she died in 1937. Carolina was only twenty-three. Without a close family network for support—her younger brother disappears from her narrative without a trace—Carolina set out for the metropolis of São Paulo because she had heard that it was a "paradise for poor people."[8] On the long walk to São Paulo she slept under bridges and in doorways. She accepted almost any job along her route but seldom was retained for very long. She cleaned hotel rooms, worked in a hospital, and hawked beer. She got jobs performing in small circuses that played on vacant lots in different parts of the city, sometimes as a singer. She would have given anything to be a performer, but that did not work out.

Being a maid was one of the few socially acceptable positions a young black woman could expect to have in the city. Carolina, however, did not last very long in the households that employed her. She explained this as the result of employers trying to take advantage of her, or distrusting a servant who read whatever she could get her hands on. Once she was fired by a white family after four months because she was too "independent" to clean up their messes. She was also a dreamer. She wanted desperately to have the life of an educated person. She envied people with enough money to buy and read newspapers. She had high moral standards and believed in the work ethic. The more she sought to be treated with respect the more people rejected her, in part because of her habit of saying bluntly what she thought. Her employers considered her cranky, and were made uncomfortable by her hunger for conversation about the events of the day. No longer did she seek the best in others as she had done while young. She withdrew increasingly into herself, cultivating annoying personal habits, including muttering to herself. She daydreamed, aspiring to become a famous writer.

Still, she refused to be docile. After her initial period of temporary jobs in São Paulo, she obtained some fairly good positions—seven in all over a period of ten years—in wealthy houses in the fashionable districts near the city center. She was dismissed, however, from each of them for one reason or another. For a short time she worked for a well-known cardiologist, Euricledes Zerbini, who gave her access to his books and who discussed politics with her. She worked for other rich people as well, for the Delamanas in their mansion and for Lucila Toledo Pisa. She claimed to have worked for General Góes Monteiro, the *eminence gris* of the dictatorship proclaimed by chief of state Getúlio Vargas in 1937 and that lasted until 1945. In what had become her trademark bluntness, she described the general as "physically repulsive but very smart".[9] She also worked for Julieta [Julita] Molina, a Spanish woman who agreed to be the godmother for Carolina's second son.

Carolina had been sexually active as a young woman although for a long time she did not become pregnant. Generally, she sought out white men for sexual partners, an attitude consistent with the repressive racial system that fostered self-hate among blacks who internalized the Brazilian tradition of considering black women inferior racially but desirable sexually (outside of marriage). With so little self-esteem, black women often vied for the attentions of lighter-skinned men, since it gave them access to higher economic levels and because the *mulato* children from such unions would have better chances in life. The unwritten rules of Brazilian society permitted this for black women, especially when they were considered physically attractive, but it disparaged unions between black men and white women except in rare cases—starting in the 1960s with soccer hero Pelé's ballyhooed marriage to a blond woman—where the black partner was a public celebrity.

Carolina surely understood society's unwritten rules as well as anyone. When her duties were finished, she would slip away at night for sexual liaisons, as did many young maids, but in her case, her forceful personality asserted itself and shaped her relationships with men. She knew each of the fathers of her children; she did not accept casual sex. She was sometimes confused by the attentions of men: she puzzled over the fact that even once when her legs were still covered with ulcers, her boss told her that he would leave his wife for her. She always displayed her sexuality openly. Elite men, after she became famous, felt uncomfortable with Carolina's sexual candor and with her independence and ambitions to better herself. They also disliked the fact that she preferred white men, and that she refused to marry.

Most of Carolina's lovers were white foreigners or naturalized Brazilians. She avoided northeasterners and, especially, blacks. At age thirty-three, in 1947, she became pregnant for the first time. She named the baby João. The father was an Italian sailor who ultimately deserted her and returned to his ship. When her pregnancy showed, her employers ordered Carolina out of their house. Unemployed, she had no choice but to build a shack in one of the city's *favelas* (shantytowns). These jerry-built slum precincts were relatively new for São Paulo, although favelas

*Carolina Maria de Jesus and son
João, c. 1949. Courtesy Vera de
Jesus Lima.*

were well established in Rio de Janeiro. In São Paulo, traditional residential patterns had altered, with the old inner city now surrounded by an affluent belt of new housing. The postwar economic boom that São Paulo experienced caused a major housing crisis as tens of thousands of families were evicted by developers who razed the old tenements and constructed luxury apartment buildings. This forced wage-earning families to move to the scattered, low-cost neighborhoods of the city periphery.[10] The fetid favela slums that were beginning to sprout on empty lots in high-risk areas provided the cheapest housing for unemployed migrants and others unable to pay for public transportation to the city center, where work was available. Carolina knew that living in these places was precarious. Officials could expel residents on the pretext of urban renewal or property owners could extort tenants by charging for water or electricity. She selected Canindé favela because it was closest to where she had previously worked and was also near a junkyard where she could forage for building materials. The favela was small—34,500 square meters—on city-owned land. It had been founded in 1954 by poor squatters driven from the center of São Paulo as part of an effort to clean up the city for the celebration of its 400th anniversary. Using scrap tin and boards she found at a nearby church construction site, Carolina built a shack with her own hands. Among Canindé's 168 structures, Carolina's was one of the smallest, four feet by twelve.

Her shack's roof leaked, rusting her pots and pans and rotting the mattress she'd found. She affixed a sack over her window for privacy. She used a rag to cover her nose from the favela stench.[11] Water poured through roof coverings whenever it rained. There was no sewage removal and, for the first several years until a second one was installed, a single spigot for the entire favela. As a result, a line formed at dawn as women and children filled their twenty-liter cans and jars. When Carolina had soap, she washed herself and her clothing in the nearby Tietê River. The river overflowed its banks every rainy season, usually in January, and inundated the favela, bringing not only mud but disease.

Social workers considered Canindé one of the most unhealthy places in the city. The mayor's office provided emergency food supplies after inundations and attempted to teach the favelados how to prevent disease but nothing was done to curb the flooding. Some residents jacked up their shacks on piles, to elevate them above the muddy streets. A city agency even offered loans to favela residents who wanted to buy houses on the outside, but few could afford to repay them. Many favela residents in the 1950s were downwardly mobile families who had previously lived in better housing but who had been forced out by urban renewal.[12] For Carolina, the favela was a purgatory from which she could escape only by clawing and scratching through the walls of poverty and ignorance.

In 1951, a Portuguese ("who was white and gave me love and money") fathered her second son, José Carlos, nicknamed Zé Carlos. Like the older child's father, this lover also soon returned to Europe. Because the boys' fathers had given some money for food and clothing, João and Zé Carlos were born in hospitals. Carolina gave birth to her next two children in her shack, aided only by a favela midwife, Maria Puerta. Maria's story was not unusual for a São Paulo favela resident during the 1950s. She had been born in the interior to a family of Spanish immigrants. At age fourteen she married and moved with her husband to São Paulo where he sought work. They constructed a shack in Canindé and lived there for fifteen years. During the time when both lived in the favela, she was one of Carolina's few friends. That Maria was able to move out of her primitive quarters to a real house was something that favela residents could aspire to in these days, and Carolina shared Maria's dream of someday leaving the shantytown for a better life.

Carolina's first daughter was stillborn. The father was an American named Wallace who may have worked for *Time* or *Life* magazine, but nothing more is known about him.[13] Carolina gave the stillborn baby her own name, Carolina, so she could save the name Vera Eunice, which she had found in a book and always loved, for a daughter who would survive. This second girl was born soon afterward. Vera Eunice's father was a Spanish-born businessman (Senhor J.A.M.V., or Manuel, as Carolina later called him in her diary), who purchased scrap paper and junk from Carolina. He only sporadically gave money for his daughter. "He didn't know for a long time that I bore his daughter," Carolina wrote later, "he has many servants and I guess that's where Vera Eunice gets her fancy ways."[14] Once when he came to Carolina's shack, a neighbor saw him and expressed amazement at his gleaming shoes. Carolina liked him because he did not care about how filthy her clothes were and said that their friendship was "as strong as the roots that hold a tree to earth." She slept with him that night in the favela—she does not say where her two small boys were—and she describes the night as "delicious."[15]

She provided for her children by continuing to forage in garbage cans for food and clothing. She was paid a few cents per pound of usable paper, glass and plastic bottles, and cans. On bad days she earned nothing and had to go through trash cans for food. On better days she earned the equivalent of twenty-five or thirty cents, enough to buy provisions. In Canindé, Carolina refused to conform to favela behavior. She considered herself superior to her neighbors. She was proud of her intelligence, and she was determined to fight until she could find a better and more moral life for her children. She steadfastly refused to drink alcohol. In her writing, she claimed to have been rejected by her neighbors because of her airs and because she could read and write. She, in turn, came to despise their behavior and what she considered to be their penchant for lying and dissolute habits. In particular, she considered "Bahians" (the general label she used for dark-complexioned northeasterners) to be violent and unpredictable. She considered herself superior because she was from Minas Gerais, a "respectable" state in the center-south and the repository of Portuguese colonial culture, even though, as a marginalized black, she shared nothing in common with the *mineiro* gentry.[16]

Carolina's diatribes against northeasterners obscure the fact that Canindé housed people of diverse racial and ethnic backgrounds. There were descendants of Italian immigrants, Poles, Portuguese, Spaniards, gypsies, and even a Japanese woman, Dona (Mrs.) Tomiko. The majority of residents were from small towns in the rural interior of the state, having come to the city in hopes of finding work, just as Carolina had done. In this sense, the slums of the industrialized cities had many residents with wider work experiences and greater ambition than those who stayed in decadent places like Sacramento, Carolina's place of birth. Many favela families were eager to send their children to school, as Carolina was, and went to extraordinary lengths to turn their miserable shacks into dignified homes. When the Tietê River flooded the favela, residents spent weeks scrubbing down the walls of their shacks, washing and drying everything. Since they owned little furniture, there wasn't much loss, but they did their best to remove mud and to maintain sanitation.

Although favelados were at the bottom of the economic scale, the cycle of favela life differed little from that in less precarious neighborhoods. Carnival in the favela throbbed with drumbeats, dancing, and liquor. Saints days were celebrated with religious processions and fireworks, especially in the months following Lent. Priests of the Order of St. Vincent came to Canindé to organize religious activities. Charitable groups distributed clothing and favelados were given access from time to time to medical and dental clinics. City officials often debated how to eliminate the favelas and, some years after Carolina became famous, Canindé was torn down. Nevertheless, a rash of new and larger favelas sprouted across the city. Politicians handed out presents for poor people at Christmas, using train stations, the local soccer stadium, and churches as distribution centers.

Day-to-day life in Canindé, however, was harrowing and dangerous. Once Carolina was stabbed five times in the leg and thigh by a knife-wielding prostitute who had chased Carolina's son João through the streets of the favela. Maria Puerta describes what happened when Carolina interceded: "I saved her. I stood in front of her and said to Ivone [her assailant]: 'If you are going to stab Dona Carolina again, stab me instead. . . . She doesn't deserve it. She works hard, she goes out to gather paper to give bread to her children.' The black woman [the prostitute] backed off and went away." What set Carolina apart in Canindé was her penchant for spending several hours a day writing. Just as in Sacramento, where she was called a witch for her habit of reading books, in the favela she earned the reputation for being eccentric. Once, Maria Puerta recalls, out of maliciousness a woman tried to incriminate her by robbing some clothes and leaving them in the ditch near Carolina's shack. The police found the clothes and wanted to arrest Carolina, but Puerta and some others intervened, talking them out of it.

Since her adolescence, she had composed poems and fanciful stories about princesses and castles as therapy to help her escape her dreary existence, and she wrote several novels.[17] She tried in vain to find publishers

and was sometimes given the names of potential editors by social workers. She showed up at the offices of editors and submitted stories and
poems; one poem, about Getúlio Vargas, was published in 1941. A reporter in 1944 wrote a story about her, calling her a "Negro poetess."
Her work was dismissed as being forced and ungrammatical. Most editors didn't even give her the courtesy of reading what she wrote. When
they saw her coming, they slammed their doors. Some called her "the
pickaninny." One editor slammed the door in her face, shouting at her
that she should write on toilet paper. Somehow she managed to send a
fiction manuscript, entitled *Clíris*, to the *Reader's Digest* in the United
States, but the manuscript was rejected. In 1941, the newspaper *Folha da
Manhã*, to whom she had sent poems, printed one of them along with her
photograph.[18]

Beginning in 1955, she began to write a diary in notebooks fashioned
from scraps of paper she found while foraging. Her diary entries, written
with a powerfully personal narrative force, reflected a mixture of hope
and ruefulness. She captured moments of poignancy with a touching
manner: once, when they ran out of things to eat in their shanty, her
daughter Vera asked Carolina to sell her to her godmother, Dona Julita
"because she has delicious food."[19] Whether or not all diaries are subcon-
sciously written for others, Carolina's handwritten diary fragments conveyed a richly-felt sense of her personal life. She was, as feminist scholars
say, "constructing a self."[20] In its confiding simplicity, it brings her inner
world to life.

Her earliest notation, for July 15, 1955, typifies her style:

The birthday of my daughter Vera Eunice. I wanted to buy a pair of
shoes for her, but the price of food keeps us from realizing our desires.
Actually we are slaves to the cost of living. I found a pair of shoes in
the garbage, washed them, and patched them for her to wear.

Carolina slept every night in her shack with a pencil and paper under
her pillow so that she could write down what she dreamed about. Her
diary mixed revulsion about her miserable life with touches of gentleness:

The sky was the color of indigo, and I understood that I adore my
Brazil. My glance went over to the trees that are planted at the
beginning of Pedro Vicente Street. The leaves moved by themselves.
I thought: they are applauding my gesture of love for my country.[21]

While Carolina always claimed to be a loner and at odds with her neighbors, a close reading of Carolina's journal shows that she was seen within the favela as a person who was stable and who could be trusted. Marta Teresinha Godinho, the social worker assigned to Carolina's family in Canindé, later described Carolina as "discreet but high strung." She also recalls that she was a striking woman. "She was very African: tall, handsome, with noble posture and very dark color."[22] Carolina was reserved except when she was angry. She was adamant about raising her children her own way. She did not drink alcohol because she feared losing the respect of her children. Some neighbors sent their own children to her to be cared for when they were released from the notorious state institution for homeless and delinquent children. Favela children were sent to this depressing place when they broke the law or simply when their parents could not provide for them. She heard their stories about conditions at this institution and fought all the harder to protect her own children from the consequences of their poverty. When there was a fight in the favela, it was Carolina who called the police (using her own coins for pay phones). In her eyes, she had a responsibility to act as an agent of stability and decency within the turmoil of the favela.[23]

Many of her diary entries reflect her bitterness at her miserable fate although she fought against despair, often completing a description of a harrowing day by telling something that had made her happy, like seeing the sunset or seeing the lights of the city at night. She wrote of death and of watching restaurant employees spill acid on garbage so that the poor could not take food. She wrote about excrement, drunkenness, sons who beat their parents, prostitution, undernourishment, and hopelessness. "Black is our life," she said; "everything is black around us."[24] She often chided politicians for showing compassion during elections and then forgetting the poor. At other times, she attributed God-like qualities to them. "I think that Dr. Adhemar is angry," she wrote about Adhemar de Barros, the mayor [and later governor of São Paulo], "and he decided to be forceful with the people and show them that he had the strength to punish us."[25] She conjured up wistful images: "What I revolt against is the greed of men who squeeze other men as if they were squeezing oranges." She reviled politicians as hungry cats among hapless birds and burned a copy of a newspaper with a picture of a politician who claimed to speak for favela dwellers.[26] On the other hand, she never lost faith completely. She spent her precious money to be photographed so that she could apply for a voter identity card, and she often got up before dawn to go and stand in line to vote so she would be finished early and then be able to go out collecting junk.

The Diary Discovered

Carolina's life abruptly changed forever in April 1958, during a municipal election campaign. One day, Audálio Dantas, a twenty-four-year old reporter for the evening edition of the *Diário de São Paulo*, arrived to research a story on favelas. Dantas had been born in the capital of the northeastern state of Alagoas. He migrated to São Paulo in the 1930s when his father opened a food and provisions store in the interior of the state. The son never formally studied journalism, but taught himself to write in a newsy style. He hustled his stories and photographs as a freelancer and eventually was hired by the *Diário* as a feature reporter.[27]

By chance he elected to feature Canindé in his story. On his first visit, Dantas wandered over to a recently inaugurated playground (granting benefits such as this had long been a Brazilian political custom). As he interviewed people, Dantas witnessed an exchange of curses between a group of men who had been competing with the neighborhood children for places on the new see-saws and swings and a tall, thin black woman. He heard her yell, "If you continue mistreating these children, I'm going to put all of your names in my notebook!" The young journalist later asked Carolina about her writing. She took him to her shack and showed him pages filled with fairy tales, fiction about rich people, poems about the countryside, and entries from her diary. There were notebooks scattered all over the shack with dated entries in them. Some of the writing was on cardboard or on newsprint. Reading the scraps of paper, Dantas found them to be, in the words of her English-language translator, David St. Clair, "crude, childlike words, much like a primitive painting done in words."[28] He recollects that after reading one page, he knew that it was important social testimony. Dantas selected one of her notebooks which covered a three-year span. At first she refused to let him take it to his editor, saying that her diary was "filled with ugly things and ugly people."[29] The reporter ignored her protest and published excerpts from it along with his accompanying story.

After this first meeting, Dantas visited regularly on weekends and brought candy and little gifts for the children and writing paper for Carolina. He spent hours talking with her about her diary entries. Everyone in the favela knew about the reporter's visits. His interest boosted Carolina's pride in her writing but angered some neighbors who thought her vain and arrogant even before Dantas's arrival in her life. Carolina basked in the reporter's continued interest in her writing. From this moment, Audálio Dantas became inextricably tied to her. "I am not bringing you a newspaper story," he said to his readers, "but a revolution."[30] The newspaper continued to print her diary fragments in a tightly edited serialized form, and they caught the attention of the public, turning Carolina into a celebrity.

In the aftermath of these events, Dantas was made São Paulo bureau chief of O Cruzeiro, a leading national weekly magazine. By this time, he had taken the role of Carolina's (unofficial) agent and mentor, and he spent a year editing her diaries. Carolina wanted him to publish her poems and short stories as well. But Dantas, a progressive reform-minded journalist, saw in her writing what he considered to be the unvarnished voice of the socially downtrodden and ignored everything but her Canindé writings. After encountering initial reluctance from several publishers, Dantas finally reached a publication agreement for the edited diary with Livraria Francisco Alves. The publications director was Paulo Dantas Neto, no relation to Audálio. The contract represented a major coup. Francisco Alves was one the oldest and most prestigious publishing houses in Brazil.[31] Paulo Dantas was himself a self-taught novelist and essayist who had achieved some importance in the literary world and was widely respected. He remembers listening to some of his colleagues at the press saying that the manuscript was a waste of time and that it wouldn't sell. Acting on a hunch, however, he convinced the business manager, Lélio de Castro, to do a run of 3,000 copies as an experiment to see what might happen. His intuition that the manuscript was something special carried the day.[32]

Paulo Dantas recalled much later that he had nagging doubts about the viability of the project and that he had told the reporter Audálio that it was not a book but a pain in the neck.[33] Then, Paulo Dantas remembers, "the television phenomenon happened," and "sales went wild." Brazilian intellectuals were not interested in Carolina's story, but television was because of rising excitement about national political reform.

News broadcasts covered Carolina extensively and she soon became a sensation. Yet on the day in August 1960 that Carolina walked out of the favela at 5:00 A.M. with her children to see her book for the first time and to sit at a table autographing, she had to sell junk she had foraged to have enough money for food and her bus fare.[34]

Carolina's 182-page *Quarto de Despejo* ("The Garbage Room") describes in vivid detail the way its author survived by picking up trash. It refers to not only to the garbage found in favelas, but the name given to a back room in many Brazilian houses, an enclosed porch, or a space under the back stoop, used for storage of junk before its disposal. In this sense, the published diary's title refers to a nondescript place in the back where castoffs and garbage were allowed to accumulate—just as human castoffs and people considered rubbish were allowed to accumulate in the growing shantytowns of Brazil's cities.[35] *Quarto* sold 90,000 copies within the first six months, making it the most successful book in Brazilian publishing history. During the height of her success, Carolina earned $60 a day in royalties, a veritable fortune for a woman who had made her living by scavenging.

From the beginning, Audálio Dantas and Carolina shared a special relationship. Neither one liked the other, but each understood that their own fortune would be tied up with the other's. Dantas applied pressure on Carolina to rewrite some entries to make them more current. He added nothing and only edited it to make it shorter and to eliminate repetition. He also toned down or edited out entries he considered inappropriate. In the published diary's preface, which he subtitled "Our Sister Carolina," he affected a patronizing tone:

> Carolina: our sister, our neighbor, there in Canindé favela, 'A' Street, Shack #9. The shack is this way, made of boards, covered with tin, cardboard and scraps of wood. Two rooms, not very comfortable. One is a living room-bedroom-kitchen, nine square meters, and a small bedroom, with just enough room for a bed. Her humanity is this: Carolina, Vera Eunice, and approximately thirty-five notebooks.[36]

He went on to say that the exterior of the favela was as ugly as the interior of her house. Carolina, the preface continues, "you shouted loudly and your shout was heard by others. . . . Your door opened. . . . You found the key to open it. . . . Favela anguish has escaped," he said, "and some people will turn away their noses because of the foul odor that escapes with your words." Forgive us, he concluded, "these people do not understand the reasons you had to open the door of the garbage dump. . . . To them I say: our sister who opened the door is great. . . . she is a small piece of Brazil." This preface did not appear in the English-language edition. Instead, the publishers printed a longer essay by David St. Clair providing biographical background for readers unfamiliar with Brazil.

What message did Carolina Maria de Jesus's first published diary convey? The entries span a long if disjointed period of time (July 1955, then May 1958 through January 1960), but the entries all fit the same model. In each one, Carolina describes in terse, colloquial language what she did from when she woke up to when she lay down to sleep. In this regard, the reader comes away less affected by individual descriptions of suffering or poverty—although these are disturbing—than by a gathering sense of the numbness of Carolina's existence. Because the diary is so personal and so filled with detailed descriptions of her hour-to-hour activities, there is little explicit political content. Carolina in her diary did not advocate resistance to the system or revolutionary action because she was too tired after each day of scavenging. She did offer specific criticisms, however, the most pointed being an indignant rebuke to the local Catholic priest, Brother Luiz, for preaching resignation and submissiveness to the poor. In her treatment of the priest, moreover, Carolina displays her unfortunate trait of distrusting those closest to her. Once when he accompanied a group of public health nurses to the favela to check residents for sores, she mocked him in her sometimes crude manner: "I'd like to know how Brother Luiz discovered that the *favelados* have physical sores," she wrote.[37]

The exhausting routines of her daily struggle made her cross and surly although she seemed to try not to let this show in her writing. She knew that she was smart, and she knew that because of a twist of fate she was condemned to life in the favela. She knew that others, less intelligent and less perceptive, occupied higher stations in life. Smarting at her circumstances, she constantly judged her neighbors and they almost always fell short. This one was a troublemaker; that one she calls a "bitch." She refused to permit people to treat her with familiarity and held herself aloof from the people around her. Her intense self-confidence and high degree of self-esteem bolstered her resolve and sustained her dignity even when

Carolina visiting Canindé after publication of her diary, 1960.
Courtesy Audálio Dantas.

women threw filled chamber pots at her children or screamed obscenities
at her. She looked down on favelados who took charity. She protected her
independence. "I never married and I'm not unhappy," she wrote. The
men who wanted to marry me "were mean and the conditions they im-
posed on me were horrible." She expressed pride in her children's self-
esteem and literacy. Her son Zé Carlos told her that he planned on
becoming a distinguished gentleman and that she would "have to treat
him as Senhor José."[38] She wrote in her diary that she hoped to sell a
book to a publisher so that she could buy a piece of land and leave the
favela.

Sometimes Carolina's diary reveals her mixed emotions. She mocked
herself because, as she said, no one expected a black woman to think or
say such things. She wrote that she was not nasty to people lest they bring
a lawsuit against her—as if any middle or upper-class Brazilian would
ever waste the time and money necessary to bring a lawsuit against a
penniless favela dweller. She satirized politicians by name, comparing their
intrigues to the behavior of favela women whose episodes of rowdyism
"grate against the nerves."[39] Again and again she declared her desire to
be left in peace, to be able to shut the door and to read and, especially, to

write. She was cleverly manipulative, zinging people she did not like, then rationalizing and backing off, retreating to her own world. "I don't resent it," she said, after a neighbor, Dona Elvira, gave her reason to believe that she had burned five stacks of her scavenged newspapers. "I'm so used to human malice." And, finally, to end her entry and to gain sympathy anew: "I know I'll need those sacks badly."[40] Elsewhere in her diary she relates the disgusting tale of a middle-class housewife who gave a slum dweller who begged for food a carefully wrapped package which yielded two dead rats when the woman returned to her shack to feed her hungry children.

While most of her stories recounted the banality of her existence, occasionally she let her spirits and her imagination soar. On a warm night in the favela, she reported, she felt the "crazy desire to cut a piece of the sky to make a dress."[41] But she came down to earth quickly. In the same entry she wrote:

> I'm not going to eat because there is very little bread. I wonder if I'm the only one who leads this kind of life. What can I hope for in the future? I wonder if the poor of other countries suffer like the poor of Brazil. I was so unhappy that I started to fight without reason with my boy José Carlos.[42]

It is the variety of her experience that distinguished her observations from mere complaints. Carolina was uneducated, but she understood the abstractions and realities that held life together. She recorded her identification card number: 845,936. She lamented a black boy's death in the favela not only because he had become bloated as if made of rubber but because she knew that he had died without having been registered at birth. "Nobody tried to find out his name," she noted. She understood full well the Kafkaesque bureaucratic web faced by all Brazilians, especially the marginalized. The Health Department, she noted, sends nurses to test for parasitic infections, but the government doesn't provide money for medicine. The afflicted are informed that they have the disease, but they are unable to cure it. Instead, Carolina and her neighbors resorted to folk remedies like garlic enemas, herb tea, and cornstarch mixed in water to fill an infant's stomach when it cried from hunger. She clung to simple (although seemingly unattainable) goals: to be very clean, to wear expensive clothes, to live in a comfortable house, to escape from the favela. Carolina's diary entries seemed to be written for comfortable Brazilians,

people who she hoped would be shocked by her descriptions of spells of
dizziness caused by hunger. At the same time, she filled her diary entries
with descriptions of her dreams. She wrote about one, after a day hunting for scrap and carrying it to the junkyard:

> I am very happy. I sing every morning. I'm like the birds who sing in
> the morning because in the morning I'm always happy. The first
> thing that I do is open the window and think about heaven.[43]

Some days later, she reported another:

> I dreamt I was an angel. My dress was billowing and had long pink
> sleeves. I went from earth to heaven. I put stars in my hands and
> played with them. I talked to the stars. They put on a show in my
> honor. They danced around me and made a luminous path. When I
> woke up I thought: I'm so poor. I can't afford to go to a play so God
> sends me these dreams for my aching soul. To the God who protects
> me, I send my thanks.[44]

A thousand people queued up outside the publisher's book shop in São
Paulo on her diary's first day of sale in August 1960. Carolina, sitting at
a table outside the store, signed 600 copies, talking briefly with each of
the people who bought one. Her former employer, Dr. Zerbini, appeared.[45]
Labor Minister João Batista Ramos told the press that she would be given
a brick house—something she repeatedly had dreamed for and written
about in her diary—by the federal government. Echoing the sentiments
of many, she replied that favelas should be eradicated.[46] In three days the
first printing of 30,000 copies of her diary sold in São Paulo alone. A
bookstore in the distant state of Mato Grosso ordered 300 copies by mail
on credit, something unheard of in Brazil. The initial volume of sales
could have been much higher but the surface of the printing press at Francisco Alves became warped, hindering efforts to turn out additional copies.

The national press's attention to Carolina in turn helped establish the
context out of which Carolina became an international success. So many
foreign editions of Carolina's diary were printed that she joined Jorge
Amado as the two most widely translated Brazilian authors. *Quarto de
Despejo* was eventually translated into thirteen languages and sold in
forty countries, including most countries of Western Europe, the Soviet
bloc, where it was very popular, and Japan. Stories about her appeared in
Europe's leading feature and news magazines—*Paris Match*, *Le Monde*,
Epoca, *Réalité*, *Stern*—and in the United States in *Life* and *Time*. Her

Carolina Maria de Jesus and children at book signing, 1960.
Courtesy Arquivo do Estado de São Paulo.

feat was astonishing: other books describing the struggles of poor Latin American women were later published in Brazil but never in the original words of an insider. These derivative books, moreover, achieved only a fraction of the audience won by Carolina when her diary first appeared.[47] Clearly, Carolina touched a nerve among the reading public not only because of what she said but also because of her extraordinary achievement in producing her diary by herself. For her part, Carolina never saw herself as a curiosity or heroine. Her testimony recorded reality as she saw it, no more, no less. The publication and initial success of her book promised financial rewards beyond her wildest dreams. Her author's contract with Editora Francisco Alves gave her ten percent of the proceeds from the sale of each book, with an additional five percent allotted to Audálio Dantas.[48] This was a standard publishing arrangement in Brazil, and Carolina was more than satisfied.

Many readers were thrilled by her story. Shortly after the publication of *Quarto*, a man of modest means named Antonio Soeiro Cabral contacted her and offered her the use of a room in the back of his house in working-class Osasco, a town about fifty kilometers from the capital. In August, Carolina and her three children moved out of Canindé with a table, two beds and a mattress, a bookshelf, and six pots. As she was moving out, her favela neighbors surrounded the truck and jeered at her. One man screamed at her that she was a "black whore" who had become rich by writing about favelados but refused to share any of her money with them. Some in the crowd were drunk. Rocks were thrown and one bloodied young José Carlos's face. Other stones struck Vera Eunice on the back and arm even though Carolina, pounding on the hood to signal the driver to leave, shielded her with her body. As they drove off, some of the favelados gave chase, brandishing clubs and throwing refuse until they neared the police post at the edge of the favela. The truck driven by a Hungarian immigrant who had volunteered his services lumbered away.[49]

Even as a favela resident, Carolina had maintained a keen interest in local politics. During the Kubitschek presidency (1956–61), politicians would frequently hold outdoor rallies where they spoke from wooden stages erected in public squares or parks. Carolina so frequently showed up at these gatherings that she became well known and was sometimes invited up to the speaker's platform to debate. This notoriety produced some benefits for Carolina. When she was stabbed trying to defend her

Moving day. Courtesy Arquivo do Estado de São Paulo.

son from attack, Carolina was sent to the municipal hospital with all the
bills paid by Mayor Jânio Quadros. On another occasion, Quadros—who
became Brazil's president in January 1961 but resigned seven months
later—arranged for her to be fitted for dentures. Carolina Maria de Jesus,
in short, commanded attention even before her diary was published. Yet
if she had not gained widespread public attention through Audálio Dantas's
discovery of her writing, she would have lived and died without any chance
of leaving the favela.

Although the politicians reneged on their promise to buy her a house,
the royalties from her book made it possible for her to have her publishers make a down payment on a house for her family. Because of the stipu-
lation in the publishing contract that she share payments with Dantas
and because of her lack of proper identity papers—members of Brazil's
lower classes often went without the documentation necessary to trans-
act business—Carolina at the time her diary was published could not
open a bank account in her own name. As a result, a trust account was
opened by Audálio Dantas for depositing her earnings. A few months

later, her publishers helped her go through the steps of signing papers to obtain a mortgage for a small house on a tree-lined street in a white working-class neighborhood (Imirim), at Rua Bento Pereira, 562, Alto de Santana, in the North Zone. Some reporters who covered her story nastily called her Santana dwelling a *barraco* (hovel), but to her it was a palace. It had a modest living room, a kitchen with a gas stove, built-in closets, a small garden, electricity, and running water. Audálio Dantas had no notion when he made the down payment that there might be people still living in the house. When the moving truck arrived, the previous owners, the Monteiros, had not yet moved out. Long experienced at living in difficult circumstances, Carolina and her children moved in to the "casa de alvenaria" (cement-block house) and, for a period of time the two families shared the house, the children playing together. A newspaper reporter recounted this with amazement: "they are cooking on the same stove, washing their clothes in the same sink, bathing in the same shower," as if such coexistence between favelados and "normal" ordinary people, as he described the Monteiros, were unnatural.[50]

Her life quickly became a soap opera. Strangers visited Carolina at all hours. Some came to ask for money. Newspaper and magazine photographers posed her in her living room seated on a sofa sewing while her daughter stood behind her and her sons stretched out on the floor reading. Vera Eunice, the accompanying story remarked, who "never liked going without shoes," now has them and someday may become a pianist.[51] Some newspaper stories claimed that the house had been "given to her by the government," which was untrue.[52] Things soon changed for the worse. Carolina and her family never felt at home in this house of their dreams. More than anything the lack of privacy brought by her fame affected Carolina. Her new neighbors, all whites, shunned her and her children. The police were called to stop fights which broke out between drunks and passers-by; the neighbors blamed Carolina for that, too. From the first day she moved to Santana carrying her possessions into the house in boxes perched on her head, Carolina knew that she would sooner or later have to leave. People pestered her for money. "What sad glory I have that does not give me peace of mind," she was quoted as saying. They make me stop everything I intended to do when I dreamed of leaving the favela. What have I become? An exploited doll and I refuse to be treated as such."[53] She told reporters that she yearned for the countryside where people would leave her alone. In the favela, she said, she had hunted for paper during the day and written for five or six hours in the evening before sleeping. In Santana she had little time for writing and felt suffocated by the attention. She became resentful, especially of people who took advantage of her and then dropped her.

Public reactions to Carolina's fame varied widely. Some journalists mocked Carolina's sudden notoriety and exaggerated her lack of sophistication. Some simply lied.

> She lives in a government-financed house in industrial Santo André and spends her days in the city, sometimes at the Fasano tea parlor frequented by the elegant people of Avenida Paulista. . . . With mascara-painted eyelashes and wearing high-heeled shoes, dressed in silk and elegant accessories from the best downtown shops, Carolina, accompanied by her three children, strolls twice weekly on Avenida Itapetininga, where *paulistas* descended from the colonial elite also walk.[54]

And:

> Playing the part of a fashion model, the formerly humble chronicler of urban misery addressed Governor Carvalho Pinto himself with a sense of superiority, according to a social columnist . . . during a visit of cultural figures to the governor's palace, she did not take the initiative to greet him. Instead, when he went over to her, at the end of the session, she said to him: 'Ah, were you here?'[55]

It may be that this conversation never occurred. Carolina wrote elsewhere of her visit to São Paulo's vice governor, Porfírio da Paz, and claimed that when she was there she felt "out-of-sorts and disoriented."[56] Still, even Audálio Dantas soon tired of her behavior. He accused her of having become "drunk with success."[57] The media continued to judge her, commenting on her manners and on her clothing. She was expected, she said later, to appear in public with docility, accompanied by her daughter Vera Eunice in a starched white dress with ribbons in her hair. She was expected to answer questions sagely in a non-provocative manner. She understood her assigned place and initially permitted her managers and editors to plan her appearances. Within a year or so of her attaining the status of a celebrity, however, she changed her mind, and refused the direction of her social betters. Growing tired of the circus atmosphere around her and the fact that she was treated as a sideshow freak, not as a serious writer or commentator, she increasingly offended those who listened to her. Progressives, who wanted her to condemn society for creating poverty, found her outspoken sense of morality and what they judged to be her innate conservatism annoying. During the military dictatorship of the late 1960s, a reporter quoted her as saying that she had read with care all of the speeches of the military president, General Garrastazu Médici, and that she planned to write him a letter telling him to provide government funds to move slum dwellers into permanent housing. On another occasion she offered praise to General Geisel, Médici's successor, telling a reporter that "he is a good man and the people like his government."[58] In an atmosphere in which radicals on the far left were engaged in kidnapping and urban guerrilla activity, her criticism of the repressive military regime was uncommonly mild. Yet her books were not reissued during the entire period of the dictatorship. Throughout this period Brazilians shied away from social issues and focused instead on the so-called economic miracle that brought great prosperity to only a few.

For her part, Carolina refused to accept that society reserved the right to grant legitimacy to some and not to others. Reformers wanted her to comment about social injustice in a broader way, asking her to relinquish her tenacious concern with herself and her children. Her unwillingness was seen as selfishness. She did not understand this criticism. Carolina would neither relax nor join others' crusades. She balked at being "handled." Her sharp tongue rapidly alienated her self-appointed advisors. It was soon said that Carolina was "unable to live comfortably with her ephemeral success."[59] Audálio Dantas, although he continued to champion her in his newspaper stories and in the introductions he wrote for various editions of her diary, more and more complained privately about Carolina's trying personality. She told people that she wanted to be a radio vocalist and after her book became successful she arranged to record a *samba* she had composed. She paid for the recording with her book royalties. She was sometimes gratified when others used her to further their goals—Archbishop Dom Helder Câmara, among others, frequently cited her to argue that the cries of the impoverished represented not communist subversion but the painful suffering of the downtrodden. But Carolina was ignorant of the unwritten rules by which public figures were expected to behave and she veered erratically out of control. The unimaginable stroke of fate that catapulted her from obscurity affected her powerfully and she seemed to crave more success. She wished to publish books and be an actress. She wanted to lead Carnival parades, just as when she was an outcast child she wanted to perform in a circus. Carolina's fanciful goals may have been influenced by her father's abandonment of her or by her mother's lack of sympathy for her intellectual ambitions, but her critics never acknowledged the traumas of her earlier life. Audálio Dantas saw her idealism and her difficulty relating to others as personality flaws. She always considered herself above the group in which she lived, he added, and this proved her downfall.

Nonetheless, her published diary contributed to new attempts to find solutions for the city's favela residents. Vargas's dictatorship and presidency (1930–1945, 1950–1954) had earlier spawned efforts to do something about urban destitution, but those experiments had been limited in scope. In São Paulo these projects typically recruited upper class volunteers to teach uneducated women, usually not from the poorest nor darkest-complexioned groups, how to sew, prepare meals hygienically, and to care for their infants. During the early 1950s, São Paulo Governor Prestes Maia was lobbied personally by the French nun and social worker, Madre Dominique, who had founded a charitable institution to provide help for the very poor. Moved by her request, he began to involve some public agencies in poor relief,[60] but in the end the movement to eradicate favelas died out. By 1970 there were far more favelas in São Paulo than ever before.

In late 1960, Carolina was sent by her publisher on an extensive tour to publicize her book. The further Carolina travelled from São Paulo the more she seemed to relax and the more she seemed able to acknowledge small pleasures. In Pelotas, in Rio Grande do Sul, on November 30th, she was given a silver plaque by the Clube Cultural Fica-Aí, inscribed "Only books make people immortal." She described her return from the ceremony to her hotel as "delicious." While in Pelotas, she observed a small house surrounded by a rose garden in bloom. "I would like to live in such a house," she wrote, simply. She constantly surprised her audiences by challenging questioners and by making statements considered provocative. Carolina in person was more outspoken than readers of *Quarto* expected. Speaking in Porto Alegre, the state capital, Carolina agreed with a black man in the audience who protested against racial discrimination. Later she was received by Governor Leonel Brizola's wife, Dona

Neuza—the "first time a governor's wife received me since I left the favela," she wrote, flattered. Dona Neuza confided in her that she hated living in the governor's mansion and that her husband, as a politician, had no friends. She offered to have her chauffeur take Carolina to visit the city's favelas, to "tell them what they need to do, that they need to study." "My dream," the governor's wife said, "is to abolish illiteracy in this state." Carolina accepted, guffawing. "The only official car I've ever rode in," she said, "was a police car."[61]

Carolina posed willingly alongside politicians and permitted herself to be used, in essence, to further their careers. At times, she seemed to be bursting with a pride tempered with wariness, offering a metaphor for others to follow as an example: "Today I had lunch in a wonderful restaurant and a photographer took my picture," she wrote shortly after she became famous. She recalled that she told him: "Write under the photo that Carolina who used to eat from trash cans now eats in restaurants. That she has come back into the human race and out of the Garbage Dump."[62] On her arrival in Rio de Janeiro, *Life* magazine sent her roses, and paid for her and her children to stay in a small room at the august Copacabana Palace Hotel on the beach. The hotel's management, Paulo Dantas confessed later, "had to swallow their prejudice against colored people" in giving her a room. To supervise Carolina's children, the hotel provided a governess, a woman from Vienna, who called Carolina "madam" and asked her where was her "companion." "Madam?" Carolina responded: "I'm from a favela and we have nothing." Zé Carlos looked out the window and said that he wanted to jump out into the hotel pool. The governess later complained about the children's brattiness, noting with indignation that they left the water faucet running.

Although the experience of visiting luxurious Copacabana as an honored guest dazzled Carolina and disoriented her, her benefactors were more judgmental. "A foreign magazine [*Life*] invited her to stay at the Copacabana Palace Hotel," Audálio Dantas said. "She went and ate in the finest restaurants. Total confusion followed. All of this in the head of a simple person, a common person; it was an exaggeration. In her head, then, it was just too much, because [her head] also contained a good, solid dose of paranoia."[63] Paulo Dantas later complained about her "terrible children sliding down the [hotel] bannister disturbing the peace," simply refusing to understand that Carolina instinctively drew her children to her as she always had done, not having relatives or baby sitters available to watch them whenever she wanted.

As a celebrity, Carolina was now free to express herself spontaneously and have her words heeded. Frequently this confused her, and she committed gaffes. In more fortunate moments things went well, and she revelled in being herself. Her publicity tour took her to Brazil's Northeast, where, in spite of her prejudiced view of northeasterners as lazy and bad citizens, she was received warmly by both politicians (notably the socialist mayor, Miguel Arraes) and intellectuals. A man in a bookstore told her that he was buying her book because he too had once lived in poverty. She was driven to Caruarú—in the interior of the state where the drought region began—and dined in silence with the mayor and nearly three dozen others at the table. She became flustered and did not remember who was the mayor. She received small gifts and visited hospitals and newspaper offices. As observant as ever, she noted that public works in Caruarú had stopped because funds had dried up.

Waiting in the Recife airport for her return flight to Rio, she overheard some people mocking her. They talked about how stuck-up she seemed and suggested her book should have been titled "From the Favela to the Moon."[64] She saw a dark-skinned woman sobbing near the ticket counter. When she inquired, the woman told her that she had come from Sergipe because her son in São Paulo had lost his wife in childbirth. She had no money for the fare to São Paulo. Carolina asked the director of the airline, Loide Aereo, who was waiting with her presumably oblivious to the scene Carolina was witnessing, to issue the woman a ticket and offered to pay for it. The agent charged the full fare, 3,700 cruzeiros, and the woman was permitted to board the aircraft. "I said goodbye to her," Carolina wrote, without asking her for her address. The incident epitomizes the conflicted nature of Carolina's personality after she achieved fame. On one hand, she remained vigilant to the suffering of others. On the other hand, her insecurity and lack of experience in dealing with authority left her vulnerable to being taken advantage of. This frustrated her and contributed to her ultimate decision to seek solace and to turn away from the public eye.

When the fanfare of her publicity tour died down, Carolina felt deflated and lonely. When she turned down persons seeking favors, some responded scornfully: "You are rich now; you have left the favela. Now

Theatrical Performance of Quarto de Despejo. *Courtesy Arquivo do Estado de São Paulo.*

you are Madam Carolina." She tried to overlook them but the words stung. Confined to the routine of keeping house, she complained that she felt that she was growing old. When reporters and television cameramen visited, she served them coffee and *pinga* (sugar cane liquor) and treated them with respect although the resulting stories often belittled her. Her neighbors scorned her, but the public's reaction remained favorable, and she continued to strive for adulation. A youth composed a samba, "Favela do Canindé," in homage. The Teatro Bela Vista presented a play based on *Quarto de Despejo*, produced by Amir Haddad. Carolina was invited to be the guest of honor for the opening performance. Although she responded that she was moved by the gesture, she quarrelled with the director and demanded that she be given the leading role in place of a professional actress. Her advisers continued to tell her what to do, and she rebelled against their advice. On one occasion, the mother of Eduardo Suplicy Matarazzo (then a student and future heir to the Matarazzo fortune and later a Senator), invited her to their home.[65] Audálio Dantas said that he counselled her not to go: "I think it is a crock (*uma merda*)," he said he told her; "you shouldn't go; they are inviting you so you can be put on exhibit."[66] She did go, however, because she was touched by the Matarazzo's warmth.

Her whirlwind schedule of appearances and interviews continued unabated. Within a year of her trip throughout Brazil to publicize her diary she embarked on a similar month-long tour of Argentina, Uruguay, and Chile. During this trip, for the first time in her life, she was free from responsibility. Her children had remained in Brazil, and she relished being able to sleep late in the morning at her hotel. Her account of this trip, in journal form, was later published as an addendum to the Argentine translation of her second diary, *Casa de Alvenaria*, issued to little acclaim by her publisher in mid-1961.[67] Outside Brazil she was generally greeted with more even-handedness than in her own country and she responded by showing a maturing ability to handle questions and to respond to new experiences. When asked by a reporter in Buenos Aires for her opinion about how Brazil should eradicate favelas, she reacted at length and with a degree of sophistication not present in her earlier discourses on similar subjects. She replied:

> Solving Brazil's favela problem should be accomplished by carrying out national land reform. This is because favela dwellers came from the countryside, where we worked as agriculturists. When the landowners did not permit us to grow food for our needs, life became too difficult. They only wanted to plant coffee. We did not receive sufficient wages to permit us to buy supplies and food. We began to suffer hunger. Then we migrated to the big cities, looking for industrial work. But we could not afford to pay high rent, and, as a result, the favelas came into being.[68]

She gamely defended her country whenever she could. "Racial prejudices in Brazil were buried by Getúlio Vargas," she declared in one interview, although her autobiographical writings were filled with examples of how as a black she had always faced discrimination. Her efforts to be a diplomat went unappreciated, however. Reports from her foreign tour in the Brazilian press belittled her as usual, despite the warm reception she received at every stop. Three thousand people attended one of the ceremonies at which she spoke. In Buenos Aires she was presented with the "Order of the Knights of the Screw," a good-humored honor awarded to visiting foreign dignitaries.

She made appearances in Uruguay and spent Christmas in Chile. Ev-

erywhere she went she autographed copies of her book. Always she wrote
a personal message in her slow neat hand. In Chile she listened to left-
wing students at the University of Concepción discuss the need for social
revolution. Later, the Communist poet Pablo Neruda came to her fare-
well tea the day before she departed from Santiago. She spent her last
hours in Santiago visiting furniture stores, wondering if she could buy
some of the beautiful metal chairs and tables that she saw. Professor Mendoza,
her host, bought presents for her and her children. She was charmed by
her foreign trip, and she returned floating on air. As usual, however, her
Brazilian mentors saw her experiences in a different light. Audálio Dantas
claimed that it only served to boost her self-delusion. "One time," he said
in 1993, she arrived "from Argentina, or from Chile" and told him that
she had met a boyfriend there, a university professor [presumably Dr.
Mendoza.] She showed him a photograph of the couple, taken by a street
photographer, one of the old fashioned cameramen who works in public
parks and who puts his head under a black cloth to take the picture.
Dantes remarked:

> You could see right away that he was no university professor. A
> university professor wouldn't have taken a picture like that. It may
> have been a joke, but that wasn't the case. The guy was some good-
> for-nothing wretch, a scoundrel passing himself off as a university
> professor or something like that. This kind of thing happened a lot.
> She had romantic expectations: she never declared any to me, but it
> was plausible that it could happen.[69]

Only a year after she became an international celebrity, public criticism about Carolina's personality flaws had outstripped expressions of
praise. Audálio Dantas's reaction, and the fickleness of the press, were
harbingers of things to come. From the beginning, critics paid more attention to Carolina's demeanor and image than to the substance of her
ideas and observations. For a brief and bewildering moment in time, Brazil made Carolina its heroine. Almost immediately, however, commentators preferred to depict her as a curiosity, not-so-subtly hinting that she
did not deserve the praise that had so briefly been heaped on her and
almost universally ignoring the issues that Carolina's writings brought
up: hunger, unemployment, racism, the difficulties faced by women, the
rigidity of Brazil's class system, the degradations suffered by the poor.
Instead, even her benefactors complained about the burden Carolina had

placed on their shoulders: "Everybody wanted to write their memoirs, to air their suffering," Paulo Dantas said, "And I had to deal with all of this."[70] The reasons for this about-face, and the rest of Carolina's story, will be told in the next chapter.

3
Cinderella Scorned

Prominent Brazilians reacted to Carolina in ways consistent with their outlook on life or their political agendas. Jânio Quadros, elected mayor of São Paulo as a reformer (and Brazilian president months after *Quarto de Despejo* appeared in print), had himself photographed embracing her. She had also been a fervent supporter of Adhemar de Barros, São Paulo's populist mayor, in spite of his open use of his office to amass great personal wealth.[1] She had campaigned door to door for him in Canindé and worked as a volunteer at outdoor political rallies in the city. They knew one another, and when they met in public they would often have a conversation. After *Quarto* was published, Governor Barros invited her to his mansion, being sure to have photographers present. She dressed up in her best clothing and exulted in his recognition of her importance. According to her son, Zé Carlos, the governor protested: "Carolina, you never asked me for anything. If you had, I'd have given it to you." Later, however, she was quoted in a newspaper story as having said that Adhemar had been responsible for the creation of favelas in her city.

Quarto received effusive praise from reformers and social critics when the book was first published. Dom Helder Camara, Recife's socially conscious archbishop, said: "there are those who will cry 'communist' when they face a book such as this." Journalist J. Herculano Pires opined: "*Quarto* is the response of the favela to the city. No one expected that the favela, sunk in mud, was preparing a response." Critic Luís Martins distanced himself from the author: "I don't know if *Quarto de Despejo* is,

65

rigorously speaking, a decent work of literature, but it is a book that leaves a mark." Others saw the work as a manifesto that needed to be read by "politicians, administrators, and candidates for political office." The writer Walmir Ayala called Carolina a "person whose viewpoint is still not corrupted." Some accepted the book without hyperbole or reservation: "it is not a work of literature, and it is not a mere denouncement," critic Vivaldo Coracy wrote: "It is a document, and, as such, has to be taken seriously."[2] Carolina received dozens of offers of marriage from admirers. She was looked at, in the words of journalist Elias Raide, as "a curious animal."[3]

Many editors and journalists during the late 1950s and early 1960s crusaded to uncover social ills and discuss the need for reform. But feature stories in the popular press and reporting on the still-new medium of television focused on personalities, not on social conditions or political issues. Topics were milked for their curiosity value and then dropped. Brazil's lack of a tradition of investigative journalism may explain why, when a marginal black woman like Carolina Maria de Jesus was discovered, she was treated so patronizingly and held at arm's-length or worse. Even when such a woman was praised, she was described stereotypically and with biting emphasis on her physical appearance. Zulmira Pereira da Silva, like Carolina from Minas Gerais, also received attention from the press in the early 1960s for her lifelong work of uncompensated charity. "Mother Zulmira" had spent most of her sixty-four years caring for the destitute in her home out of her meager resources because, as she was reported to have said, "I cannot leave anyone to die outdoors and to be devoured by vultures."[4] Nevertheless, there was always an edge of condescension in stories about her—the news stories constantly referred to her as "black and fat"; "the goodly black woman;" "the old black woman." The implication was always there, even if faint, that only an eccentric would choose to care for people who otherwise would have died in the street.[5]

The year 1960, when *Quarto de Despejo* was published, saw unusual national pride and optimism about Brazil's future. Carolina's diary became a sensation because it had been written by a candid, self-taught woman who refused to play by the rules and who demanded the right to dream of elevating herself and her children on her own terms. The message not only of *Quarto* but Carolina's later writings was deeply personal. Carolina did not call on the urban poor to challenge the system. Her books were not manifestos, and most of the urban population was either illiterate or too poor to buy her book. Hunger and her constant struggle to find food for her family were Carolina's main concerns. Other aspects of her personality and value system reflected these conditions. She was privately religious and her writings are filled with references to the Bible. Yet her relationship to God was personal, and she almost never attended mass. Like many poor Brazilians, she mixed spiritism with Catholicism, and the Catholic Church of her country was an aloof institution, like the government. Each was severely limited in its ability to help her and her family, and when assistance came it was intermittent and inadequate. This was one of the reasons that Carolina distanced herself from her world, relying on herself to maintain control over her existence.[6]

If Brazilian critics dismissed her as a shooting star without enduring importance, positive reaction abroad to her work continued unabated. In the United States, *Quarto* appeared under the title *Child of the Dark* published by E. P. Dutton in 1962. Progressives, concerned about the legacy of underdevelopment in the Third World, saw her diary as an insider's view of what Oscar Lewis would later call the "culture of poverty."[7] Reviewers lauded the importance of *Child of the Dark*, calling it "immensely disturbing" and adding their analysis of the causes of the conditions Carolina de Jesus described to the debate over the ways to combat hemispheric poverty in the spirit of the Kennedy administration's Alliance for Progress. In the following year the book appeared as a paperback published by the New American Library. It has been in print continuously since then, although its trade imprint has changed to Penguin USA. Eighty thousand copies of the American edition were sold during the first few years and at least 313,000 paperback copies in the decade following publication.

In Germany, Christian Wegner in Hamburg acquired the rights to publish *Quarto de Despejo* from Liepman AG in Zurich, a publisher who had worked as a subagent of Catalina W. de Wulff of Buenos Aires. The diary appeared in 1962 and soon became a best-seller. There was a second edition in 1968. Wegner also signed subcontracts with West and East German publishers: with Deutsche Buchemeinschaft (November 1962), Fischer-Bücherei (July 1964) and twice with Philipp Reclam Junior Leipzig

(March 1965 and May 1970). From 1983 through 1991, Lamuv Verlag GmbH in Göttingen, a leading liberal publisher, issued six editions.[8] The total number of German-language sales probably exceeded 70,000, although in the case of the two editions published by Reclam Junior Leipzig, little profit likely was made, since the house's paperback books sold for the extremely low price of two East German marks, the equivalent of well less than a dollar. The German case illustrates the fact that Carolina and her family received little or nothing from the many successful foreign translations of her books. She was not robbed, per se; her Brazilian publisher, which held the rights to foreign editions, did not realize the impact the book would have internationally, and they sold the rights cheaply. Vera Eunice de Jesus Lima claims that over the years only the Americans and French paid any royalties at all to her mother.[9]

The European editions of the diary used Dantas's introduction to the Brazilian original, the sensationalist "Our Sister Carolina." Readers in Europe reacted the same way as had North American readers: they were shocked by what they read and considered Carolina a heroine. In 1975, West Germans produced a documentary about Carolina's life, but vehement protests from Brazil's ambassador to West Germany resulted in the film not being shown in Brazil. Carolina was, however, paid $2,500 for the film rights. Brazil's Globo television network broadcast a less-controversial documentary about Carolina after her death, but it raised little interest in her writing or her story. Many Brazilian intellectuals still resented Carolina's success abroad because they were embarrassed by her and because they considered what she wrote harmful to Brazil's image. *Quarto*, writer Carlos Rangel claimed, was a "kick in the stomach of the literary establishment of New York and Paris." Like soccer star Pelé, Rangel added, "she is the perfect kind of hero for the North Americans: she came out of nowhere to achieve glory and fortune." Ironically, Rangel misunderstood the foreign reaction. Carolina's writing was never considered as literature; her writing was acclaimed for what it revealed about the nature of Third World poverty and its author celebrated for voicing what foreigners saw as an eloquent cry for help.

She was honored in Brazil as well. She was invited in 1961 to participate in a writers' festival and book fair in Rio de Janeiro, where she quarrelled with the popular novelist Jorge Amado, whom she accused of slighting *Quarto de Despejo* so that he could sell his own new novel,

Carolina at São Paulo Academy of Letters. Courtesy Arquivo do Estado de São Paulo.

Gabriela, Cravo e Canela. She and Paulo Dantas joked about this when they saw long lines queued up to buy Carolina's book. They said, "Good bye Gabriela, so long Gabriela."[10] Carolina was named "honorary citizen" and given the key to the city. Four months after *Quarto* was published, she was honored by the *paulista* Academy of Letters and the University of São Paulo Law School. When she arrived early at the Academy building for the ceremony, she was turned away at the door by the black porter because he did not believe that a black woman had business there, even though she dressed in fashionable clothing she purchased on the elite Rua Augusta. It was difficult, however, for her to overcome her awkwardness in public. "She would go out like she was, a ragamuffin with that scarf on her head," recalled Alcidez Fernández, who ran a book and newspaper kiosk in downtown São Paulo. "When she went like that," he surmised, "she thought that a favelado had always to be a favelado, right?"[11]

Only one group of contemporaries received her as a role model rather than an oddity. This was the small group of educated blacks in São Paulo, the Niger Circle, heirs of the Frente Negra (Black Front) of the 1930s. They were black writers and intellectuals who during the 1960s published a small magazine, *Niger*, addressed, in their words, to the "Negro Collectivity." Invisible to the mainstream white cultural elite of the city, this group humbly and graciously honored Carolina and placed her photograph on the cover of its September 1960 issue.[12] In the photograph, she is looking at an open copy of her book held in her hands. She appears calm but not at ease. In another photograph of her taken in the house of black cultural writer José Correia Leite's in August, she also appears extremely self-conscious. Whenever she faced a camera, even among sympathizers, her characteristic self-pride vanished and she seemed docile. These were symptoms of how strange and terrifying this new world seemed to a woman who scant months before had rummaged for garbage and collected scraps for a living.

Shortly after her diary was published, José Correia Leite, a veteran militant of the tiny movement for black recognition in São Paulo and the founding editor of *O Clarim* (1924–32) and the editor of *A Alvorada* (started in 1945), invited Carolina to his birthday party lunch at his home. He had earlier met Carolina for the first time while she was walking on Rua Augusta with the black poet Emílio Silva Araújo. Carolina arrived for the lunch at Correia Leite's house with Audálio Dantas. In making small talk, Correia Leite revealed to Carolina that his house badly needed plumbing repairs. She responded immediately that as soon as she got enough money from her royalties she would pay for the work. Dantas, playing the role of Carolina's protector, said that this was not a good idea, and told the black journalist to counsel Carolina to forego letting "ridiculous things go to her head." Correia Leite, a cautious man, took Dantas's side. He confided to Carolina that Dantas was giving her good advice, and she promised to listen to him. Correia Leite soon became critical of her personally and chided her for appearing at Carnival in her "eccentric" chicken-feather costume and for getting involved with men.[13] In the pages of *Niger*, she remained a heroine, although Correia Leite's memoirs do not say anything about the reaction of the men and women in his small circle of intellectuals to Carolina's subsequent fate. Not a single newspaper report or biographical item about Carolina mentioned her reception by her fellow blacks. The number of blacks who had reached the status of intellectuals was so small in Brazilian society that it is no surprise that this aspect of her career was ignored.

Late in 1961, less than a year after *Quarto de Despejo* catapulted its author to national fame, Carolina's editors at Francisco Alves published a sequel to the first diary, a compilation of a year's diary entries from May 5, 1960, five months after her last notation in *Quarto*, to May 21, 1961. This companion volume, *Casa de Alvenaria: História de uma ascensão social*, described her "brick house" (the book's title) and her "social climb" (its subtitle). *Casa*'s format was the same as its predecessor, but Carolina's observations (and the tone of Audálio Dantas's preface) seem a bit strained. "This is a more fascinating book in some ways," he argued hopefully, "because although Carolina no longer writes with an empty stomach, she observes distress on different levels."[14] Critics did not agree, however, and the book neither sold as well as the first nor garnered much attention. Readers were apparently tiring of her metaphors and her preachiness. Still, the publishers sold out the first run of 10,000 copies, and a second edition printed on newsprint sold almost 90,000 copies. Like the first diary it was translated into several foreign languages (Spanish, French and German but not English) and was well-received in Europe where *Quarto de Despejo* had been an enormous publishing success.

Carolina's second diary continued Carolina's story, from her departure from Canindé to Osasco and then to her brick house in Santana. Because she was more relaxed while writing it, *Casa de Alvenaria* reveals more about Carolina personally than her first diary, which dwelled on her tribulations. She credits her hard work and her knowledge of reading and writing for freeing her from the favela, and she turns to boasting. In one entry she brags that she has hired a white maid, a woman who is ashamed to be working for a black, even a famous one.[15] *Casa*, written after her Santana neighbors had rejected Carolina and her family, was more aggressive than *Quarto de Despejo*. It lacked, in Paulo Dantas's sarcastic words, "the prestige of misery."[16] In *Casa*, Carolina adopted a somewhat more confrontational style. Although this was the common discourse of white-complexioned radical students and intellectuals, it was not seen as acceptable from a black woman lacking public manners. In *Casa*, Carolina blamed politicians for neglecting the poor and even found fault with reformers, including Miguel Arraes, Dom Helder Câmara, and Leonel Brizola. By the late 1960s, Carolina was now seen in some right-wing circles as a communist, an advocate of strikes, and someone who (dangerously) quoted from President John F. Kennedy.[17]

What stood out the most in her second book was Carolina's continued insistence on fighting her battles alone. A woman who never knew her father and whose mother and grandfather died when she was young, Carolina's personality was scarred by the burden of her having to fend for herself in a hostile world. One entry after another shows her in adversarial relationships with virtually everyone she met. By 1961, if anyone supported her emotionally, or offered assistance to help her deal with the emotional whirlwind created by her sudden rise to fame, she never acknowledged it. More insecure than ever, seeking flattery but not knowing how to react to it or how to behave with strangers, the diary account of her life outside of the favela contributes little to our understanding of her inner self. Her entries do little more than chronicle her activities. They do not discuss the embarrassments she must have experienced. At banquets, for example, she sometimes ate with her fingers, as favela dwellers did. Journalists chastized her in print for lacking social graces.

By the time her second diary was published, Carolina's behavior had alienated many of her closest benefactors. She complained in *Casa de Alvenaria* that Audálio Dantas tried to control her life although she also called him her "guardian angel" and admitted that she felt comfortable at his side.[18] She accused him later of having altered her prose so much in the books which followed *Quarto* that all of the "pretty" phrases had been taken out. Dantas roundly denied these charges, asserting that in both diaries he had only improved her prose. As is apparent in *Casa de Alvenaria*, he edited out some statements, leaving the telltale ". . ." that indicated his interventions. These abridgments were especially heavy in the section where Carolina talks about Dantas himself. Yet he permitted some of her criticisms to stand in print. In *Casa de Alvenaria* she wrote that he gave the impression that she was his slave. For his part, Dantas always complained that Carolina was a difficult person, nasty and aggressive. He acknowledges that, in his words, Brazilians' "middle class social prejudice" often made them recoil when they interacted with her. Most took what they could from her and turned away. "Damn, here comes that black woman again to piss me off," he recalls his counterparts saying.[19] Neither literary scholars nor social analysts after 1961 gave Carolina credit for talent or for social significance and as time passed hardly any positive comments appeared at all. Carolina's celebrity was all but obscured by the time of the armed forces' overthrow of João Goulart's

popularly elected government in 1964. The repressive atmosphere in Brazil under the dictatorship (1964–78), moreover, dampened the kinds of
discussion of social injustice that had dominated public discourse during
the heady years of Brazilian democracy between 1955 and 1964. A critic
in 1975 dismissed her published work as a "failure" in the marketplace;
another called it a "pastiche of earlier-described woe."[20]

On the other hand, during her years in the public eye, foreign reviewers treated Carolina with respect and praise. Her accounts of her pathetic
life moved them and they found in her a ray of hope. They praised her
writing for its exposure of social misery. *Newsweek* called her first diary
a "desperate, terrifying outcry from the slums of São Paulo . . . one of the
most astonishing documents of the lower depths ever printed." The New
York *Herald Tribune* called it "a haunting chronicle of hunger . . . a dramatic document of the dispossessed that both shocks and moves the
reader." *Horizon*'s reviewer said that the book contained "the seldom-
told truth which inspires in some compassion, in some revulsion, and in
others revolution."[21] *Life* magazine devoted a full page to her; *Paris Match*
ran a longer story.[22] Novelist Alberto Moravia, in his introduction to the
Italian translation of *Quarto de Despejo*, contrasted Brazil's natural beauty
with the ugliness revealed by Carolina's diary, calling her the product of a
"caste of pariahs" as damned as untouchables in India.[23] In his prologue
to the Casa de las Americas edition (1965; reprinted 1989), the Cuban
Mario Trejo called Carolina a conscience, visionary, and the creator of a
"subliterature rising out of the soil of underdevelopment."[24]

Casa de Alvenaria was translated in Argentina as "Hunger is Yellow"
(*La Hambre es Amarilla*). In Japan, at least three editions appeared of a
translation by Nobuo Hamaguchi, a professor of Portuguese literature at
the Tokyo University of Foreign Studies. Hamaguchi was sent a copy of
Carolina's book by a Brazilian friend who was an employee of IHI-Ishibrás,
a Japanese firm. His abridged translation included only part of Audálio
Dantas's preface but included some material from the book's publisher,
Paulo Dantas; many diary entries (mostly from 1958 and 1959) were omitted from the Japanese edition.[25] In all, *Casa de Alvenaria* second diary
sold modestly around the world but it had little of the impact of *Quarto
de Despejo*.

Carolina published three additional books, one of them posthumously.
She also wrote a novel about her grandfather, *O Escravo* [The Slave], but

it never appeared. Zé Carlos, her son, later asserted that Carolina mailed the manuscript to an American publisher but never received a reply. *Pedaços da Fome* [Pieces of Hunger] was published in 1963, a kind of fictional soap opera sermonizing against society's privileging personal wealth over education or refinement, and depicting men as vain and malicious, especially male rural migrants in her words "seduced by the city." Unable to convince her original publisher to do any more of her books, Carolina turned to a less prestigious publisher, São Paulo's Editora Aquila. Her new publisher tried everything to make the book succeed, but without any luck. The cover featured a drawing of a poor young girl holding an infant: both seemed to be more Caucasian than black. The introduction was written by Brazilian poet Eduardo de Oliveira and there were four pages of critics' excerpts extolling Carolina's first book. They included the popular Brazilian novelist Jorge Amado, an [unnamed] editor from E. P. Dutton in New York, the French critic Roger Grénier, Nobuo Hamaguchi, author of the preface to the Japanese edition, a Dutch critic, the Finnish Eva Vastari, and a Swede.

No publisher was willing to take her fourth book *Provérbios* [Proverbs], a collection of pearls of wisdom and homespun homilies such as "Only the strong know how to overcome the vicissitudes of life." In 1965 she paid for it to be published out of her other royalties.[26] The book was awkwardly written and not very original. Its reception may also have been injured by the fact that it appeared in the second year of Brazil's military dictatorship, a dour period marked by social tension, although it probably would have fared badly even in more open times. *Provérbios* was dismissed in the press without further comment as the work of "Carolina Maria de Jesus, writer from the favela."[27] Her work was no longer a novelty, the market for it had vanished.

In 1982, five years after Carolina's death, a French publisher issued a fifth and last book pieced together from manuscript fragments she had given to French reporters who had come to visit her. A Spanish-language translation was published in Madrid by Ediciones Alfaguara, S.A. The text was not published in Brazil until 1986 and received almost no attention.[28] The Brazilian edition was titled *Diário de Bitita* (Bitita's Diary, from her childhood nickname). In it, she finally realized her dream of writing about her childhood in the countryside. The autobiographical book's revelations about her life in Minas Gerais were stunning, filled with nuanced detail about her experiences of poverty and racial discrimination. Some anecdotes were couched in humorous terms. For example, she described the visit of her dark-skinned uncle to a photographer's studio. The portrait came out black with only the man's white suit visible. He refused to pay, protesting that "I'm not as black as this."[29] The book ends by thanking God for protecting Carolina, even as a child, and repeating her requests from her favela days that she be permitted someday to buy a house and to live in peace.

Although the writing in *Diário de Bitita* was explicitly autobiographical, the book's Brazilian publisher, Rio de Janeiro's Nova Fronteira, classified it as fiction.[30] Minas Gerais during the early 1920s provides the setting. There are short sections about childhood, family life, being poor, about Carolina's relatives, especially her grandfather, and about illness and work. There was even a chapter on "the laws of hospitality." The writing is chatty, precise, and clearly expressed. The book is upbeat in the same unsettling manner as *Quarto de Despejo*: statements of anger and descriptions of difficulties caused by poverty or misfortune are often followed by positive references, as if Carolina wanted to draw back from harsh judgments. "I knew my brother's father," she writes, "but I never knew mine. Does every child have to have a father?"[31] Not only did she describe her day-to-day life, but she commented on social customs as if she were an anthropologist. Any black can be a beggar in the countryside, she explained in one comment, but in the city, the government "requires beggars to carry a metal tag with a serial number granted only after a medical examination to prove disability."[32]

Racial identity is one of the recurrent themes in *Diário de Bitita*. It devotes an entire chapter to "Negroes." Carolina begins by recounting a story of being caught picking fruit from a neighbor's tree. Dona Faustinha, probably a light-skinned *mulata*, confronted her by calling her a "black vagabond." Carolina retorted, cheekily: "Whites are also thieves because they stole blacks from Africa." The neighbor looked at Carolina with "nausea." A war of insults followed, centered around Carolina's self-identification as a daughter of Africa and as a descendant of slaves. The narrative then turns to a discourse on work habits. Whites, Carolina asserted, are calmer than blacks, she says, because they are more economically secure.

"In 1925," she notes, "schools [in Minas for the first time] admitted black children. When these first black school children returned home, they were sobbing. They said that they did not want to return to school because the white children said that blacks smelled."[33] Several paragraphs attacked teachers as prejudiced and lamented that Brazil's abolitionists never finished their jobs. Then, as was her habit as a writer, she pulled back, as if she was afraid of offending her readers's sensibilities since national myth claimed that race discrimination did not exist. Brazil's blacks, she claimed, had made great progress since Abolition, citing the example of Patrício Teixeira, a samba composer, and Azevedo Costa, a black physician with his own clinic in Uberaba. Overall, though, her book offered devastating opinions about Brazilian race relations almost never seen in print. She praised Italians for hiring blacks and for letting them dance with their daughters at Saturday parties. She described black laborers who earned nine *mil-réis* a day but who willingly paid twice as much to sleep with white prostitutes because, in the men's words, "no one should die without having sex with a *branca* [a white woman]." She went on to quote another black man: "You see how the world is getting better, we blacks can sleep with whites. Equality is coming."[34] She offered advice: "Blacks should not kill whites. Whites should not kill blacks. Blacks and whites have to dance around one another in a minuet."[35]

Carolina, while proud of her race and African antecedents, also commonly repeated colloquial beliefs about blacks being lazy, incompetent, and prone to drunkenness. Blacks run from the police, she writes, "like cats running from dogs." All of her writing was consistent in this regard: when she discussed the impact of racism on her life and the life of her family, she provided unambiguous, harrowing detail; however, when she talked about broader racial issues she lacked the intellectual and critical skills to get beyond stereotypes. Her observations about race vary between accurate commentary and gossip. *Diário de Bitita* reproduces jokes Carolina overheard spoken by old blacks commenting ruefully and with cynicism about the "nineteenth-century emancipation" of blacks. *Mulatos*, she explains, treat blacks disdainfully because they are so proud of their lighter complexion. Black men should not impregnate white women, she observes, for "the mulatto child will turn against the father." She recounts stories of her relatives ordered out of line while waiting for water and, upon refusing, being called "dirty blacks.".

Carolina's frequent allusions in her writing to historical events affecting race relations apparently made readers nervous because she was unlettered and many of her interpretations seemed naive. Although educated Brazilians, overwhelmingly white or light-skinned, engaged the race topic frequently, many felt uncomfortable when Carolina, a black, offered details contrary to the way things were supposed to be. In *Diário de Bitita* and *Quarto de Despejo* Carolina commented on the act abolishing slavery in 1888, saying that despite legal emancipation whites still treated blacks as slaves and inferiors. She spoke passionately about Zumbí, the leader of the fugitive slave refuge at Palmares "who sought to free the blacks." Some of her images hit home. Blacks, she said, "adored Tiradentes [a precursor of Independence] in silence." For blacks, she said, "he was the messenger of God."[36]

Carolina did not hesitate to write about the haughty and overbearing way men treated women during the period of her childhood. She wrote about the male practice of exposing themselves to women and to young girls and about other forms of sexual abuse. She observed how women feared to confront these men, taking refuge instead in deeply-held religious beliefs, seeking divine intercession. Her view of the world, of course, reflected her limited education and experience. She relied on the events in her life and on aural culture. She cataloged and described the world's ostracized races through her own personal filter: blacks (hated because of their color), gypsies (for being thieves and wanderers without a country), and "semites", because they fought against Christ. Given that Jesus pardoned Jews, she asked, why then do Christians continue to harbor resentments? When she asked an immigrant from the Middle East who was eating a *kibe*, a cooked meat patty brought to Brazil by Arabs, whether he was a "Turk" (*turco* was the popular name for all people of Levantine origin), he replied that he was Syrian, not a Turk, and that Turks were good for nothing. She sympathized with immigrants, and laughed good naturedly at their idiosyncracies.

Downward Spiral

In 1964, photographs of Carolina with a burlap sack on her back foraging for paper in the streets of São Paulo appeared in the press. Audálio Dantas insisted vehemently that these scenes were contrived by Carolina to call attention to herself and gain sympathy. Carolina had contacted tabloid reporters, Dantas said, dressed herself like a rag picker, and then posed. Carolina later denied this vehemently; she had been forced, she said, to scavenge because she had run out of money. News of Carolina's return to poverty did get out and briefly created a flurry of negative publicity for Brazil in the United States and in Europe. Partially in response to the news about Carolina's fate, a television production team in New York hoping to produce a documentary film on Carolina as part of the United Nations' International Year of the Woman commemoration took steps to locate Carolina and to interview her, but nothing came of the project.

In 1970 Carolina had left the Santana neighborhood with her children and moved farther out to the southern periphery of the city of São Paulo, to the district of Parelheiros, near Vila Cipó. For her this was the "countryside," although it was little more than a gritty, mostly barren area threatened by encroaching industrial construction. The city was moving nearer and nearer as the economic boom of the period of the military dictatorship matured. Alcidez Fernández, the newspaper vendor who remembered her from her days signing copies of her book near his stand, later described it as "the boondocks." Some wealthy families lived in the hills of Parelheiros, but the lower elevations were occupied by the poor. It was here that Carolina hoped she could find solitude. Unhappy in Santana from almost the first, she made up her mind about leaving when she overheard her publishers say that they would hide money promised for her from an Italian film production company because she would only squander it. She resolved to take charge of her life and to get out from her patronizing benefactors.

Using money from the royalties paid by her American publisher, the initial advance from the Italian film company, and the proceeds from the sale of her Santana house, she bought a wooded located near a brook. There she and her children constructed a temporary shack without electricity, just as she had done when she moved to Canindé. They slept on the floor until the municipal government sent a truck with her possessions from Santana. At the beginning, short of cash, she often rode two hours by bus to downtown São Paulo to collect paper and bottles to sell. When some foreign royalty checks arrived, Carolina purchased cement blocks and, sometimes hiring others to help, eventually built a sturdy house on her property.

Parelheiros was as close as she could get to approximating the countryside of her childhood. Her son João convinced her to open a street-front grocery where she sold liquor and foodstuffs. She commonly offered credit to local residents when they had no money. Because they rarely

Carolina Maria de Jesus in front of her house in Parelheiros.
Courtesy of Arquivo do Estado de São Paulo.

paid her back, she did not make any profits, and the store inevitably failed. When João was called into military service, Zé Carlos—then nineteen—managed the shop. During this time, he started to drink heavily.

Domestic newspaper stories described Carolina's plight but in a disparaging tone that depicted her as a fool for having sold her house in Santana. When the foreign press picked up the story, at least one Brazilian newspaper reacted by expressing irritation at the fact that outsiders still though Carolina worthy of praise. Rio's *O Globo* quoted an American student, Robert Crespi, who had written to Carolina on Harvard University stationery, in a "mixture of Portuguese and Spanish," asking her if the story of her newly lowered standard of living was true. He was quoted:

> I have just read the English translation of *Quarto*. I have never read a better book about Brazilian life. I have heard that you are back in the favela. This life of hunger and survival is sad; I do not understand why you had to return. I hope that you can soon take your children to a better place . . . [but] I don't know how one escapes from this kind of life. You may write to me if you wish. . . .[37]

She spent much of her time reading the daily newspaper and cultivating corn and other garden crops. She complained that her gardening efforts cost as much as they yielded and that her efforts to sell produce by the side of the road came to naught.[38] She also continued to write, starting a novel about upper-class life, *Felizarda*. She did not cultivate companionship with her neighbors except for a woman known simply as Mariazinha. Her one friend from Canindé, the midwife named Maria Puerta, lost contact with her until the mid-1970s, when she visited Carolina's family in Parelheiros "out in the country."

At times she spoke optimistically about her future. She had, after all, achieved a meaningful step upward from the favela. Interviewed by a reporter, she said that she hoped to enlarge her house, build a water tank for irrigation, and expand her garden. She had come to live, in the journalist's words, on the level of the "typical poor Brazilian *caboclo*" [settler; also denoting mixed-race], a pejorative term used in this instance to emphasize both her lack of manners and her rustic life-style.[39] Carolina's Parelheiros house sat on a parcel of land adjacent to an unpaved road. Visitors walked on boards over dust and mud to enter the pumpkin-colored house with green window frames. The press later said that Carolina called her house the *Chácara Coração de Jesus*, the "Heart of Jesus garden," a pun on her name, but Vera Eunice later denied the report, suggesting that journalists had invented the story about the name for ironic effect.

She marshaled her day, in her son's words, "like a sergeant." Vera was just like her, Zé Carlos said, working tirelessly by day, attending school at night. Carolina delivered avocados, bananas, and manioc from her garden to a woman who sold it for her at a market. Carolina also raised chickens and pigs. When she had spare cash, Carolina bought colas for her children or took them to the movies. Their lives were difficult, but they lived much better in Parelheiros than in the favela. Still, this improvement in the family's condition was far below the level one would expect of an author whose books were still selling well in more than a dozen foreign countries.

As she turned fifty-seven years old in 1970, Carolina continued to fight for herself and for her children. Sometimes flights of fancy caught her. She wrote to politicians in the time-honored Brazilian tradition of *pedidos*, letters asking for personal favors. She wrote to the governor of Goiás in the remote interior to ask him for permission to live among the

Indians there. This she said would allow her to divide her Parelheiros property among her children. The letter was leaked to members of the press, who then ridiculed her.[40] Slowly, the flurry of sensationalism that had followed revelations that she had moved away from Santana subsided, and Carolina went on with her life.

Critics and journalists still considered her a curiosity. In 1976, Carolina was interviewed by Neide Ricosti of *Manchete* magazine, one of the two most popular magazines in Brazil. The journalist emphasized Carolina's personal bad luck and unpleasant appearance. "With mud-covered feet, badly dressed, and disheveled," she wrote, "the ex-favela dweller lamented that the worst thing that had ever befallen her was to have written four books." As earlier, Carolina was blamed in elitist and racist terms for being who she was. "The surprising success that had yanked her out of misery," the article pontificated, "was too heavy for [her] . . . almost primitive upbringing."[41] The reporter described for her readers the "discomfort and slovenliness" of Carolina's house on its "tiny plot of land." On the walls, the article said, were yellowing photographs, "demonstrating that times had passed, fading, as well, one's illusions." Electricity had been hooked up in 1974, and there were two television sets, one owned by her son João, who lived with her. No copies in Portuguese of *Quarto de Despejo* or *Casa de Alvenaria* were on her bookshelves, although they contained copies in the languages to which her diaries had been translated.[42]

The reporter criticized Carolina for being conceited and quoted her wistful statement that once she had purchased beautiful clothing at São Paulo's Bela Itália emporium. Yet it is clear that Carolina herself made light of the matter by adding with a wide smile that "both the store and I are finished." Carolina spoke in a firm voice, Ricosti observed, and made eye contact "from bottom to top" of the person with whom she was speaking to look them over. "A bit distrusting," the reporter added; "she resists talking about the past." "I don't dwell on those days," Carolina was quoted as saying; "Things were very confused. I didn't understand what was happening to me. I went to Chile, Argentina, Uruguay . . . [as for] friends [they] come only when one has money. With poverty, everyone disappears."[43]

According to Ricosti, Carolina said that Parelheiros was a good place because it allowed her to "eat vegetables, kill a chicken, make soup." As

for what made her happy, she replied that she "now had clothing to wear."
The *Manchete* reporter then quoted Carolina at length:

> If I had to write *Quarto de Despejo* now, I wouldn't. I was very
> rude. . . . The book was a disaster for my life. . . . I wrote influenced
> by hatred, hunger, misery, in the harsh atmosphere of the favela. I
> was a kind of a witch. It was hard to live in that atmosphere. In
> Brazil, there is no need to have that type of place: there is so much
> land. I don't know how people carry on there. People who live in
> favelas totally lack culture. A cultured person, one who doesn't get
> drunk, who reads, who behaves, who doesn't steal from employers—
> doesn't live in favelas. This is what my grandfather said; I wrote it
> down.[44]

The last article about Carolina to appear in the press was both terse
and patronizing. The *Folha*'s headline read "Carolina: Victim or Crazy?"
When the reporter Regina Penteado arrived unannounced at Carolina's
house, Carolina, she wrote, greeted her with a "grunt." "The woman
who taught the Argentines [about Brazilian favelas] and who dreamed about
stars" Penteado wrote, "met us [at Parelheiros] wearing a pink dress covered with dust. Her legs were covered with ordinary stockings, a clear
dark beige, with blue and white tennis shoes." Carolina's garden plot, the
reporter conceded, was well tended and the ground swept, "with the ex-
ception of one spot covered with a piece of newspaper which apparently
had been blown there by the wind." The house's main room with its
cement floor, the article said, was messy but clean. There was a bookcase
with mostly "very old" copies— Victor Hugo's *Les Miserables*, Machado
de Assis's *Quincas Borba*, and Euclydes da Cunha's *Os Sertões* [in
English, *Rebellion in the Backlands*]. Carolina Maria de Jesus, best-selling author, was being judged by a newspaper reporter on how she coordi-
nated her wardrobe and kept house. Was the reporter implying that erudite
books in the house of an ex-favela dweller were inappropriate? The cap-
tion to the photograph published with the story read: "[Carolina's] ideas,
her complaints, her delirious head continue the same as ever."

By December 1976, the date of the interview, two of Carolina's children, Vera and Zé Carlos, had married. Zé Carlos and his first wife had
three children. The reporter described Carolina's four-year-old granddaughter as a "light-skinned little *mulata* with a runny nose." Late in the

questioning, which lasted several hours, Carolina, who had always tried not to express bitterness when being interviewed, lashed out at "all of the Brazilian and foreign publishers" involved in her work. She showed a notebook to the reporter, saying: "This is my way of getting back. I have terrible poems in which I will seek my vengeance. Here in this notebook I have all of my grief."[45]

Carolina had attempted to find peace in Parelheiros but her life remained stressful. Now in her sixties, her always volatile temper had shortened even further. She was no longer the handsome woman she had been. She was wizened, stooped, and painfully thin. She argued constantly with her children, especially Zé Carlos, whose personality, of the three, was closest to hers. He later claimed that these shouting matches were a form of education for him, but her disappointment in his behavior and his refusal to accept her direction are clear. The passing of time and the burdens of her life were wearing her out. Still, Carolina remained alert. When she watched television and read the newspaper, she would be filled with ire about the continuing deterioration of slum conditions, about high infant mortality rates, about pollution, and about other issues of the day. She was never really happy, her son said in a letter to a São Paulo magazine, but "she never made a big thing about it in her life."[46]

Carolina's last opportunity to regain public recognition for her writing occurred in December 1976. Edibolso, a São Paulo publisher, bought the rights to her first book from the original publisher, Editora Francisco Alves, which had fallen on hard times. The new publisher made arrangements to print a new low-cost edition of *Quarto de Despejo* aimed at the popular market. The repressive atmosphere of the military regime had begun lifting and publishers were more willing to release books on issues of race and poverty. After the Edibolso edition appeared, Carolina was invited to sign copies at bookstores and newspaper kiosks on the Viaduto do Chá, São Paulo's main artery, at the Shopping Center Iguatemi, and at the craft market at the Praça da República, as well as other important places. She did the same in Rio de Janeiro, autographing books downtown and in Copacabana. She signed each book carefully: "With affection, Carolina Maria de Jesus," or "God will guide you." Briefly, Carolina exhibited excitement about the prospects for further attention to her book, first published sixteen years earlier. Some of the autograph sessions were filmed and broadcast over television.

Carolina signing copies of new edition in 1976. Courtesy of Augusto Nazário.

At the time of Carolina's last book-signing sessions, journalists reported that a film version of *Quarto de Despejo* would be made by a studio in the United States. The producers sent her money and she bought new clothing for everyone; Carolina travelled to Rio de Janeiro for a week to confer with the film's agents. She thought that she was going to be flown to the United States—although she was probably misinformed. She told Zé Carlos that she wanted to play herself in the film. Negotiations stalled, however, when Edibolso, which owned the rights to her book, demanded a larger fee. Negotiations failed and Carolina earned nothing.[47] A delay in the filming schedule ensued, and Carolina died before anything was resolved. The film was ultimately abandoned.

Published reports about the amount of royalties received by Carolina varied widely. A Rio de Janeiro newspaper story asserted that through March 10, 1961, *Quarto* had earned for Carolina Cr$6,000,000—worth the equivalent of $31,579 at the beginning of 1961.[48] In addition, Carolina continued to receive small payments in dollars—in one case, $300— from her American publishers. Carolina ceded her rights to authorize foreign translations to Editôra Paulo de Azevedo Ltda., a branch of Francisco Alves. There was nothing improper about this—it was standard publishing practice—but the result was that she received very little in foreign royalties.

She had been, of course, able with her initial proceeds to buy the brick house of her dreams. We do not know for sure where the rest of her royalties went. She probably lost money on the sale of her Santana house when she moved to Parelheiros. It is also possible that she may have been overcharged for her plot of land in Parelheiros. She bought furniture, television sets, things for her children. Carolina also lost a good deal of money on the phonograph record she had made. She paid all the production costs and lost her investment when the records failed to sell. After she became famous, she was accused of spending extravagantly on clothing. But Carolina had always led a disciplined, modest life, and it is unlikely that she squandered all of her royalty income. Nevertheless, many Brazilians examined her difficulties through the distorting lens of race prejudice. One of her editors supposedly told her it was "pointless to give anything to a Negro who behaves like you." From the time her first book was published, she complained that others were collecting royalties due her; however, she offered no proof of her allegations.[49] Audálio Dantas later accused her of squandering her money on men.[50] Dantas claimed that, like the French writer Colette, unscrupulous lovers took advantage of her. There is no evidence of this, and her children deny the allegation.

Carolina's Death

During her last years, in the middle 1970s, Carolina's self-imposed isolation increased. The flurry of activity over the republication of her first diary subsided, and her trip out of the country never materialized. Vera remained dutiful, but she was married and no longer lived at home. João, who suffered from ill health, held various jobs; Zé Carlos was with his wife and family. Death came to Carolina Maria de Jesus at the age of sixty-three on February 13, 1977 in the midst of a scorching summer. The obituaries either said that she succumbed to emphysema or an attack of acute asthma. Her children later denied that she suffered from any respiratory ailment; they did not know why she died. In any case, by the late 1970s, her neighborhood of Parelheiros had become polluted in its lower elevations as the result of its proximity to massive industrial plants. In her last years, Carolina appeared frail, more like a woman in her eighties than a sixty-year-old. Experiencing difficulty in breathing, she had taken a bus to her son Zé Carlos's house and declared to her daughter-in-law Joana that she had come there to die. After arguing heatedly with José Carlos about many different things, she suddenly stopped and said that she was feeling worse. He refused to believe her and did not call a physician. Joana later claimed that Zé Carlos, from whom she was estranged, shouted at her: "Go ahead and die, then!"[51]

When Carolina's condition clearly worsened, a neighbor agreed to drive her to the local first-aid post. But the neighbor took a long time getting dressed, and Carolina died en route. There was no money to bury her. Her children, saying that they were penniless, appealed in the press for financial help.[52] Finally, Carolina's one close neighbor friend, Mariazinha, paid most of the costs for the casket, the wake, and the funeral. Audálio Dantas attended the service and years later claimed to have arranged for the wake and paid for the burial. Carolina's children, however, deny this emphatically. The district's mayor donated a stone marker for the grave. During the service, the priest remarked during the mass that no one had brought flowers. The mourners in response went out to the gardens on the grounds of the church and cut blossoms to scatter over the gravesite.

Few people understood Carolina during her final years. In keeping with the harsh judgments nearly always expressed about her personality, the obituaries in the Brazilian press blamed Carolina for having failed to adjust to success. They claimed that she was unable to develop beneficial relationships with the "right" people and she was too proud to play by the elite's rules. Rio's *Jornal do Brasil* obituary was typical in being neither terribly sympathetic nor accurate:

> Carolina Maria de Jesus, the author of *Quarto de Despejo*, died yesterday . . . as poor as she had been when she began to write the diary which would turn into Brazil's all-time best-seller. . . .[53] Her book royalties allowed Carolina, in 1961, to purchase a brick house, a symbol—as she often pointed out—of her personal victory over hunger and misery. But her second book failed to attain the popularity of the first, and she began to quarrel with her friends and supporters, including the journalist Audálio Dantas, who had discovered her scavenging for paper on which to write her diary, and who had acted as her agent.
>
> Little by little, Carolina began to lose the resources which her book had brought her. She purchased everything in sight: she visited the famous, frequented the salons of the rich—but in time she began to

irritate her hosts. . . . Her inability to adjust to success cost her dearly. . . . Forced to sell her brick house for non-payment of debts, she relocated her family to a rural shack along the Parelheiros road. There she raised chickens and pigs and lived in poverty, refusing, however, to become a burden on her now grown children, It was in this place that she was found yesterday, dead of an attack of acute asthma.[54]

When her body was discovered, the mayor of nearby Embú-Guaçú offered a valedictory. She was buried in the cemetery at Vila Cipó, a polluted industrial suburb near Parelheiros, the place to which she had escaped to in search of fresh air and seclusion.

João José, her hard-working and loyal eldest son, died of renal failure a few months after his mother. Dr. Zerbini, the surgeon for whom Carolina had worked as a maid before entering the favela, performed a kidney transplant at no charge, but it was unsuccessful and João's life ended three days later. After her mother's death Vera rented out the Parelheiros house to tenants. Vera had become a teacher in the local public school while her mother was still alive. She studied English at night at a technical school and later matriculated in the local Faculty of Letters in a training program for English-language translators. Zé Carlos, twice divorced, now lives in nearby Vila Cipó. He sees a woman who in 1992 gave birth to a son, Jonas. His two former wives live in poverty with their children. Chronic alcoholism keeps him from working regularly, although he is hired to drive a truck from time to time. He is angry and unpredictable and although obviously intelligent, cannot hold a job. When he is working, Zé Carlos lives in a bleak, windowless room alongside a noisy highway. When he is too drunk to hold a job, he sleeps under highway overpasses or in a favela.

Cinderella Scorned

Clearly, Carolina was held to a higher standard than others, probably because she was a feisty, opinionated black woman with a too-honest tongue. Many observers condemned her for failing to have transformed herself into a docile, well-mannered member of the middle class. This was unfair. The circus-like atmosphere surrounding her moving to the Santana neighborhood doomed any possibility of sympathy from her neighbors. Moreover, Carolina and her children, fresh from the favela, were unskilled in the middle-class deportment expected of them. Carolina understood that the demands placed on her were unreasonable, given her schooling in deprivation. Her last years in Parelheiros were trying ones, but they provided her the gift of command over her own life. She spent much time with her friend Mariazinha. A number of Catholic priests in Parelheiros occasionally visited and discussed her writing. She welcomed their contact, and it may have revived Carolina's religious self-identity.

In spite of Carolina's great achievement in taking control of her life, some observers never forgave her behavior. A 1992 conversation with a Brazilian Northeast-born intellectual (whose anonymity needs to be protected) sheds further light on the ways that some members of Brazil's elite perceived her. The speaker took pains to emphasize Carolina's hatred (his word) for the common people. He also noted her jealousy, her quest for fame, and what he called her bruised psychology. "The Frankenstein which we created," he added, was "a monster we didn't know how to destroy."[55] Ignoring the role of racial and sexual discrimination and the cupidity of others in Carolina's incapacity to cope with the demands placed on her, he attacked her for aggressiveness. When she died, he remarked, "her kids were relieved because she was a hindrance." He blamed, as well, the publishers who brought out her later books, the company that issued her samba recording, and Audálio Dantas himself, whom he called ambitious and "a touch shady." This allegation was unfair to the journalist who discovered Carolina. Without him, her diary would have never been published. He never enriched himself from Carolina's fame, although he was in a better position to capitalize on the success of Quarto than Carolina. He went from the diary to the prestigious national magazine O Cruzeiro and in later years was elected head of the Brazilian Association of Journalists and to the São Paulo legislature.

This anonymous source, who was close to Carolina when she was a celebrity, explained that he expected her to be able to think and react the way Brazilians with more "proper upbringing" did. She was "a lot of work, psychologically and psychiatrically speaking," he said. "When you abolish the dream world of a neurotic person," he adds, "they turn against those close to them." Carolina's fame disoriented her, he said, and disturbed her mentally. "She wasn't normal," he recalls, "and because she wasn't normal she wrote what she did." Carolina, this observer noted, "had the essence of suffering, humility, and she wanted it all because she wanted a life she couldn't have, like a Cinderella, a fantasy."

Foreigners were less concerned about the nuances of Carolina's personality and overlooked her flaws. They read in her narrative a sweeping condemnation of Brazilian society that Carolina herself never directly intended. *Quarto* lamented the system that had produced misery and racism, but she offered no prescriptions for its reform. Non-Brazilians, however, clearly saw in the published diary what Carolina herself had only conveyed with ambivalence. The American author of the unproduced screenplay about Carolina, for example, declared that Carolina embodied "a fierce indictment against political corruption and an account of the sordid life of the favelados."[56] Meanwhile, the Brazilian Left, including members of the various branches of the Brazilian Communist Party, rejected Carolina as an aspiring bourgeois—which in some ways, with her intense personal work ethic and traditional values, she was. Yet the Soviet bloc idolized her and *Pravda* once interviewed Carolina at length about her feelings after being hungry for days at end.

Brazilian reviewers commenting on her writing disparaged Carolina's talents to the end of the life. Before she died, some of them commented on the fact that her grammar was improving, but they attributed this to her daughter Vera's help. One reporter complained that Carolina's improved "erudition . . . manifests itself [in] a certain mental confusion [that] perhaps robs her of the authenticity she showed in the favela."[57] We should not be surprised that Carolina made progress in her writing. She always had worked hard to improve herself, and she bought a dictionary, desk encyclopedia, thesaurus, and daily newspapers. Few were willing to acknowledge this. Her discoverer, Audálio Dantas, said later that she "was a person subject to highs and lows," and that this likely resulted from "a process of insanity, or mental overexertion, brought about by all of the misery through which she had passed."[58]

Carolina Maria de Jesus's short-lived fame in her country among affluent Brazilians during the early 1960s reflected in part a growing awareness of social problems and poverty. Most of them viewed the underclass in either the idealized terms of a revolutionary vanguard or as a source of violent and dangerous behavior. The initial public receptivity to Carolina's story was to some degree part of a new romanticization of the life of the lower classes by middle and elite readers who hoped that the traditional docility of the poor would be preserved. This also explains the elite's acceptance of popular music that praised the simplicity of the *povo* [the common people] in the lyrics of the Bahian composer Dorival Caymi and

Members of Guarujá Women's Association. Photo by Flávio de Souza Brito.

others later on. Another example of this romanticized vision was the French-made film *Black Orpheus,* which employed handsome black actors and a lush musical score to depict favela life. In the film, Rio's favelas were picturesque, sanitary neighborhoods, devoid of mud and affording panoramic views of the city.

After 1964 the military government's emphasis on civic and patriotic education helped to preserve Carolina's memory, albeit in a minor, sanitized way. Some officially sanctioned school texts, following the regime's new emphasis on portraying Brazil as a melting pot, recalled Carolina as an example of a "notable woman" who had become an author and who had written about urban problems. Ironically, these references disappeared when democracy was restored in the late 1970s. They were most likely dropped because the civilian government sought to downplay the military regime's rhetoric about patriotism, national unity, and racial harmony. In greater São Paulo the only legacy of Carolina's 1960 rise to fame was a mayor's office decree to name two small streets after her, one of them in Parelheiros. A municipal school and an infant nursery (*creche*) were also named for her. In 1990, in the town of Guarujá, near the port city of Santos, a group of eight or nine lower-class women, two blacks

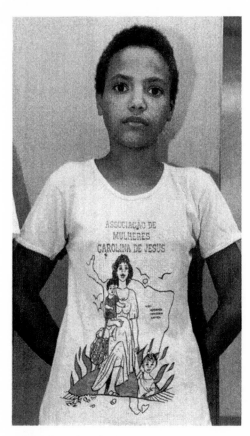

Ze Carlos's daughter wearing Guaruja Center T-shirt. Note the idealized depiction of Carolina, who, despite standing in flames, has the appearance of a suburban matron. Photo by Robert M. Levine.

and the others light-skinned migrants from the Brazilian Northeast, voted to name their new women's center after her. The center's first director—a social worker—had provided three names to choose from, and they had selected Carolina's; they even took to calling themselves "Carolinas." When first queried about what they knew of Carolina Maria de Jesus's life, her namesakes replied simply that she had been a black woman who had become famous.

Virtually all the reviews and commentaries that appeared in print in Brazil from the publication of *Quarto* to the time of her death evaded the issues that Carolina wrote about: poverty, race, hunger, religious faith, food, medicine, single-parent families. One after another, reputable critics focused on Carolina herself. At best they painted her as a curiosity and at worst as a scold and a nuisance. What Carolina suffered at the hands of the Brazilian establishment was also experienced by many if not all pre-feminist female authors on socially controversial subjects. What was unusual in Carolina's case was the near total absence of even grudging acknowledgement of her relevance as a social critic or as a voice articulating the condition of the poorest members of society. Commentators and critics of every ideological position simply ignored her. She was unimportant. It was as if Brazilian academics, journalists, writers, and politicians had closed ranks in shared hostility to her lack of political correctness.

After more than fifteen years without any editions of Carolina's books available to the Brazilian public, two publishers recently issued new editions of *Quarto de Despejo*. A small edition was published in 1991 by a mail-order club. The other was a 1993 edition of the diary by Editora Ática of São Paulo, an edition designed to appeal to a young persons' market. The cover—drawn by an artist in an idealized manner—depicted a handsome black woman and three children, draped as if statues. Editora Ática also published a supplement for teachers that offered questions and answers about the book.[59] A national newsmagazine ran a story about Vera and Zé Carlos. The diary sold fairly well and awakened a new awareness of Carolina Maria de Jesus. Despite this significant first step, it remains to be seen whether a new generation of Brazilians will consider her story instructive.

Vera Eunice de Jesus Lima still possesses some of her mother's manuscripts, including parts of unpublished novels and a variety of unfinished poems. The family archive also contains some of Carolina's original diary entries. However, Audálio Dantas insisted on keeping the notebooks that were used in the production of her original diary. The notebooks, each filled out in a flowing and careful hand, are falling apart from age and humidity. There are also clippings, letters, photographs, fragments of manuscripts, and memorabilia. There is a blurred photograph of Carolina and Vera in their spotted chicken feather Carnival costumes, like their mother's, sewn painstakingly by Carolina. Vera recalls that some years ago representatives of a planned black culture museum spoke about housing her archive, but nothing came either of the suggestion or of the museum.

Poor black women have remained at the very bottom of Brazilian society, but at least one black woman from the slums—Benedita da Silva, the daughter of a washerwoman born in a Rio de Janeiro favela—ran for mayor of the city in 1992. She lost by a margin of less than 100,000 votes to a conservative white candidate running on a mildly progressive platform. Some commentators recalled Carolina's origins and referred to Benedita da Silva as "Rio's Carolina Maria de Jesus." The lives of the two, however, were different on every level but the poverty of their youths. "Bené" da Silva, an Evangelical Protestant with a charismatic personality, has devoted her life to the political cause of the poor. As the first black woman elected to Congress, in 1988 she was the primary advocate for the inclusion in the new Brazilian Constitution of an article criminalizing racial discrimination.[60] Carolina, on the other hand, exhausted by her long personal struggle and the needs of her family, never saw herself as a champion for the rights of others. When asked for an interview, the mayoral candidate (and Brazil's lone black woman member of the national Congress) replied by requesting that Carolina's books be sent to her. No one on her staff had ever heard of Carolina de Jesus.

Why did Brazilians respond so warmly to Carolina in 1960 but hardly respond at all to the publication of new editions of *Quarto* in 1993? There are many possible reasons, but the most likely is that the tenor of the times has changed. Carolina's diary appeared during a time of optimism in Brazilian life when educated Brazilians thought favelas could be eradicated through social and political reform. Book buying habits, too, changed. Brazilian bookstores carry far more foreign books in translation today. Readers now prefer books that address important contemporary political issues, particularly what happens following the failed administration of Fernando Collor de Mello, who was forced to resign in 1992 following a corruption scandal that implicated him personally.

Canindé was one of only less than a dozen favelas in São Paulo in 1960. Three and a half decades later, millions of destitute people lived in shantytowns and slums that sprawled across the metropolitan landscape. Canindé itself was razed to make room for a modern stadium, home to the elite Portuguesa soccer club. By the 1990s, in most cases conditions were far worse than those described by Carolina a generation earlier. Many urban residents, including children, were homeless and forced to live in cardboard shelters under the open sky or under bridges. Drugs and violence now infest the city's slums. In the 1950s, alcohol and unemployment were serious problems. Yet many favela residents like Carolina dreamed of leaving and many succeeded. Today, faced with corrupt and ineffective governments, political and economic instability, uncontrollable inflation, noise, pollution, recession, and rising crime, many educated Brazilians had become inured to the suffering of others, and were uninterested in Carolina's story. They were not interested in hearing about race discrimination, or the travails of impoverished women, or about misery. They had constructed walls around their lives, sealing off their families in wealthy residential compounds guarded night and day by armed men. For many who did remember Carolina and were sensitive to her plight, the world she described seemed increasingly dated. For them *Quarto* had become a historical document rather than a commentary on current problems.

4

Carolina's Children

Research for this book took many forms. It included reading and analyzing Carolina's published and unpublished writing, including manuscript fragments and typescripts prepared by Vera from her mother's handwriting. It also involved locating articles and other sources about Carolina's life in newspaper files ("morgues") and archives, communicating with her publishers and agents, finding out what critics said about her outside of Brazil, and, most important, conducting the in-depth "life story" interviews described in the first chapter. Comments from all of the interviews were used in writing the narrative chapters, and the two most important interviews, with Carolina's surviving children, Vera and Zé Carlos, are transcribed here. They offer loving details about their family's life and testify to their mother's strength and her ability to influence her children despite a life almost continuously afflicted by deprivation.

Vera Eunice de Jesus Lima, b. Canindé favela, São Paulo, July 15, 1953. Interviewed at her home, São Paulo, November 14, 1991 and subsequent dates.*

My name is Vera—Vera Eunice de Jesus. I also am Vera Eunice de Jesus Lima; Lima is my husband's last name. I confess that sometimes I

---

* Those readers who wish to see the text of the original transcripts, in Portuguese and with pauses and skips noted, should consult *Cinderela Negra,* the Portuguese-language version of this book.

Vera de Jesus Lima. Photo by Robert M. Levine.

forget this; I get confused. It's been this way since my mother was alive. Carolina Maria de Jesus! Carolina, my mother! Anyone who remembers the 1960s will remember her. For me, she represents very much, very much indeed! Her story has to be known. She—my mother—was poor, very poor. She lived in the favela and went hungry, but she finally realized her greatest dream alone. Without anyone's help. She wanted to be a writer, famous, to have her name printed on the cover of a book. She battled extensively and devoted her life to her goal. There is no one in the world I admire more than her. All of us have our defects, and she also had hers, I know. She was a difficult person to live with, but who isn't? For a favela dweller, don't you think this was enough, what my mother did? . . . more than Jorge Amado, imagine!

Our life changed immensely after my mother became successful. We were invited to parties in mansions, we travelled. My brother Zé Carlos even once sat in the lap of the governor of São Paulo. We left the favela and went to live in a house constructed of bricks. It was a real house, with a refrigerator, beds . . . a fine house; it looked like the one I live in now. [If] it weren't for my mother, for her help, bringing us to school, today I would be still living in a favela. For this, during my entire life—my "life history," as you say, is thanks to my mother. She suffered far more than she should have. She was born poor, but she fought, fought more, *fought* . . . she wrote books; she became famous, but she died forgotten. In spite of this, during my entire life she was a good mother to me and my brothers. From the days we were in the favela, when we had nothing and lived dirty because we had no running water, even then we had more than other poor children.

We lived through many difficult times. Life there was hard because of the violence in the favela. It was especially hard for children. If the home wasn't violent, the street was. Poverty was responsible. Children went to school because fathers were unemployed. If you went to school, it was to have lunch there, not in order to study. My brothers and I studied a little because my mother worked a lot, the whole day, for us to have some food in the house to eat: bread, rice, beans, whatever we could get. Sometimes there was nothing and we went to bed hungry. She would say: "Hunger is the worst plague of the favela." It's true! Without food, children lose the will to play, they become weak, they fall sick.

My father? I never knew him, and I don't want anything from him! He's already dead, but he always knew he was my father, that we were miserable, and he never did a thing for me. He was rich, imagine! Owner of a factory! . . . and he never gave the least help to his daughter. Our life is odd, isn't it? My mother was a destitute favela dweller but she fought for us to have a better life, to leave the favela. My father, an industrialist, filled with money, never paid for me to go to the dentist . . . nothing! If today I am a teacher and a university student, living in this house, whom should I thank? Not him, who never assumed the smallest responsibility. It seems that he never even wanted to meet me. I owe everything I have to my mother's help, to my husband Paulo, and to my own efforts.

My mother never let us leave the shack because she worried about what would happen to us. If she went out, she would take all three of us. She scavenged everything you could find in the street . . . she scavenged

all day for paper, bottles, cans. She took us with her wherever she went
... with me on her shoulders, with João and José walking along, we
spent the entire morning walking the city streets. It wasn't easy, it wasn't!
We went from block to block, passing by abandoned buildings, to be able
to sell the junk at the end of the day and to buy food with what we got. I
am very proud of this, of what she did for me. I am proud and respectful
too. My mother would work the entire day, with great hardship . . .
beyond this, there was nothing—*nothing* else she could do to survive. It was
a struggle! Favelados awoke at dawn and went to sleep late at night. And if
they refused to carry out *one order* of their employer, they would be fired just
like that. What kind of work? Ah! Whatever had to be done, whatever . . .
they did this, or they died of hunger. You couldn't choose. The jobs they got
were the worst kinds of jobs available in those days. My mother worked and
cleaned as a maid when she was very young. She cooked, ironed, took care
of children, all of this in exchange for practically nothing, a slave's wages!

Her attempts to study were worse, even harder for her than being alone.
The people where she lived could not accept a woman who studied, read
the newspaper, and talked about what she read with men. Here's where
the pot boiled: a Negro, a bastard, wanting to mess around with learning
about things? It was the end! [In Sacramento] . . . they didn't even let her
enter the church. It ended up becoming impossible for her to live in Sacramento because there were no jobs. Like many poor people from northern Brazil, my mother went to the big city to better her life. It was the
only way. [Her] first months in São Paulo were even more difficult. She
didn't know anyone. She had never left her small town, and now she had
gone right to one of the largest metropolises in the hemisphere. In time,
living virtually without food, things began to improve. She got work . . .
as a maid, washing the floor in a restaurant, cleaning dishes, and if you
do well enough the boss asks you to come back. In this way things improved for her. Suddenly, even rich families were willing to hire her! You
see? She had nothing, was alone in the city without a cent in her pocket,
but she tried hard and never refused an offer of a job. She did good work,
and besides, was personally clean and knew how to talk to her employers. She was not a stone without any culture, someone who automatically
accepts everything. She wasn't! When she cooked, ironed, waxed . . . she
did everything very well, and she knew how to talk to the people in the
house, something even more important.

My mother never lost the habit of reading and writing, which are acquired while young. And if she had on the tip of her tongue the events of the day from the newspaper, if she had read novels and poetry, then why not become a writer? She wrote, submitted things to the newspapers, and sometimes got published. She *loved* it! She'd put the clippings in a folder which I still have today. One of the oldest is a clipping of a poem written for Getúlio Vargas, whom she admired deeply. My mother had her good moments in those days. She had to work a good deal, but on her breaks she could read and write. And there's more: my mother began to have boyfriends! If this didn't happen in Sacramento, here it did. She . . . she was some lover! She adored making love and being infatuated. To be charming—it was a serious business! Her preferences were odd: she didn't like to be involved with [native-born] Brazilians, especially Bahians. And, if he was black, get out! She wouldn't go near Bahians or blacks, even as friends. She was sure that Bahians were worthless, irresponsible, and lazy. Although I am married to a very hardworking man [a Bahian], I realize that Bahians in general, like the *cariocas* [residents of Rio de Janeiro], love to sit at the beach all day. I only don't understand her prejudice against blacks. She was her father's color, pretty black! Why, then, this problem with black men?

In the favela we didn't have better financial conditions than the others, but few people got along with her. With men she was involved with, the situation was worse. My mother was fussy about the men she went with. If she didn't like them, even if they pursued her it wouldn't do any good! When we were in the favela there always was some man impassioned with her, who wanted to marry her. Sometimes they would argue publicly, right in front on our shack. Marry? Why? To become dependent on a man? Then she threw the man out. I saw how ferocious my mother was: she refused to marry, and she only went out with gringos! Do you know that each child had a different father? She assumed responsibility for all of them: alone, poor, but she took care of us. If my sister Carolina hadn't been born dead, we would have been four. Only two of us are alive today, me and Zé Carlos. João lived with us for a long time but he died shortly after my mother, when he was in his twenties. Almost no one knows that my mother gave birth to Carolina. The father was an American named Wallace . . . an American, mind you! It was a long time ago, and even we never learned about him.

My mother used to tell us about each of our fathers. She would say who they were, what they did, where they were. We never met them face to face. What I remember most about them was the countries they were from: the United States, Italy, Portugal and Spain. Mine was Spanish. My mother's greatest love was the Portuguese father of Zé Carlos. Ah! that Portuguese!. When she spoke about him, she breathed deeply. João's father was a drunk. My mother, who never drank, threw him out. I think he never knew that he had a son. I was the last to be born. My father was a well-heeled Spaniard, the owner of a factory where they made scales and a paint company. My mother was already living in Canindé when she met him. After spending the day scrounging for junk from the street, she would go to his business to see if he had any old paper to give her.

It was because of these romances that she began to lose her jobs with the families who had hired her. They didn't like it when she went out at night during the week. She came in at all hours. When she became pregnant, then, it was the last straw. The families liked her but they preferred to hire single women, childless. Even today, in the neighborhood where I live, there are many women who know this dilemma: when they work for families some of them have abortions so they will not be fired. The well-off people don't want the expense. It's incredible, but it is reality. Only my mother didn't accept such things. In no way! She left jobs before she was fired from them. If her employers grumbled, she found another job and left right away. Her life was hers! With children, things were looking bad for her. One small child, a second, and my mother no longer gets anything. She ends up going to the favela.

The favela is the first thing that I remember. It was where I was born. Everything was dirty, filthy, and every shack was overcrowded. During the night there always was some kind of commotion outside. My mother woke up, told João to watch us, and went to see if she could resolve the problem. I lived fewer years in the favela, but of the three of us, I'm more of a favela product. My mother always said this. João and Zé Carlos were born in hospitals, with a doctor, nurses. They weren't born in the favela. We only came here later. I was born inside our shack. With me there was no doctor, no nothing. I was born in the hands of a midwife, Maria Parteira [Maria Puerta]. Every month new families arrived: father, mother, children . . . they found the least undesirable spot and suddenly another shack appeared. From night to day the population grew. One shanty smaller than the next, and filled with more people. I still remember these images, a little place to live, with floors of beaten earth, a stick of furniture in the corner, a table, the rest crates and tin . . . from this came the name *Quarto de Despejo*, my mother's most famous book. It was called the "Garbage Room" because it was the place to throw the things no one wanted. Canindé was like this, a space to forget the people who weren't worth anything any more.

Most of the things I remember about the favela—the garbage, the violence, the hunger—still are nightmares for me. That is how I see the favela, as a nightmare following me. I still remember that school was the only source of food for us during the day. We did have food, but at least once a week we went without. These days I still awake sweaty during the middle of the night. For a child, especially, the favela experience is traumatic! I never have been able to blot it out. Some nights I have nightmares. I dream that I have returned to that suffering, chaos, and misery. This is the reason that I still feel sorry for people who live in favelas . . . if you haven't lived in one, you can't imagine what it is like. My mother detested having to live under those conditions and to see her children deprived of necessities. It was worse when she hadn't been able to find anything. Our money wasn't enough to buy a bread roll. We went to sleep and when we woke up, she hadn't closed her eyes. She was so worried. She tried. She was willing to walk from early morning to nightfall in the street . . . to be able to bring food home. Even so, we were hungry.

Soon after I was born, during the 1950s, my mother began to write her diary. During her sleepless nights she would take a used notebook and write down things that had happened. She wrote about the people in the favela, about the police, who had been fighting, who died . . . everything that happened in the favela and to us was written down. My mother did everything possible for us to remain outside of the favela most of the day. School, the movies, the park, she sent us all over, anywhere, as long as it was not in the favela. The money for this? We didn't have enough money to buy proper food, but my mother wanted us to stay out of the favela! She disliked not only the favela but the people who lived in it. When João and Zé Carlos were little, they would go to hunt for paper. Later on, my mother gave them money to stay away the whole day. They only returned at night, to sleep. Movie tickets ended up costing much of our money for food, but she preferred it that way. She preferred to leave at dawn, with her sack on her shoulders, to walk, walk, walk and to go to bed hungry, rather than to leave us alone in Canindé.

Does this explain why this story is half mine and half my mother's? Our lives were always close. We were a closed family inside the favela. After, when the money from the book came and when we went to live in a house in another neighborhood, we stayed together . . . always together. In the favela we were dependent on my mother, and we shared a tiny space within the shack. Rarely did we play outside. After the book, we suddenly had a house, we had friends from high society, the press. Carolina Maria de Jesus was the person of the year after the book came out! Inside our family, our relations with others didn't change much . . . whether in the favela or in the middle class neighborhood, a wall separated us from others: my mother. Today, when I have time, I sit with my children and tell them the story of their grandmother.

Audálio Dantas, a journalist, discovered my mother. He entered our lives at the end of the decade of the 1950s. I was still a child, but I have various press stories from these times that my mother cut and saved. Audálio had gone to the opening of a little park in the favela, but it had been taken over before the children could even play there once by troublemakers and vagrants, who set out to break the swings and other things placed there! My mother called the police, and the press found out, and Audálio showed up. The bums were in the park with my mother on the other side of the fence, shouting loudly: "I'm going to put you in my book!" This is what gained the attention of the reporter. He asked to read the notebooks, picked out the most legible parts among her pages and pages of diary notations, novels, and poems . . . and took them away to read. He came back later and told my mother that a newspaper would help her publish her diary, only the diary! Not any of her novels or her poetry. Audálio told her to continue to write, telling about the events in the favela, about poverty, the fights, and they would try and find a publisher. My mother, naturally, became wildly enthusiastic! She wanted to write a book and see her name on the cover.

We knew Audálio as "the reporter." On weekends he would show up at the shack to visit us. He brought new notebooks for my mother and candies, sweets, chocolates for us. We were little. Imagine what a party we had! My mother said that he was very busy. She said this because as soon as he arrived, he left. Sometimes they sat down, the two of them, on the boxes and spent hours talking. In the favela, they thought that she was crazy, walking with her notebook under her arm. There were people who laughed. The worst ones laughed at her piles of paper, but they stopped when they realized that it was neither a joke nor craziness. When Audálio came, everyone paid attention. They stood watching the "newspaper boy" who only came to talk with Carolina. When he said that the book was almost ready to be published, our situation became even more complicated. My mother became more anxious: everything she talked about was "the reporter" and her book. She talked of nothing else. We received clothing, news of which spread like wildfire in the favela. Everyone knew about the book. My mother's friends came to visit, to find out what was happening, and her enemies became more nasty than ever, out of jealousy.

During these days, Audálio was preparing and editing the text. The work to select the best parts took a long time. "Everything can't be in the book," he would say "I had to correct the parts that were confusing and to lighten up the parts that were too serious." Some of the stories he removed out of fear that the public would be offended or that the publisher would change his mind. My mother continued to write about what was happening and never worried about what was proper or wrong. In fact, I still remember an episode that no one knows about; it didn't come out in the book but it is in the original in one of the notebooks Audálio took. The story I am referring to happened to me, and I'll never forget it. It was a shock. I was playing on the grass in the favela, late in the day, in front of our shack. My mother was inside with someone visiting her. I played with bottles, pieces of wood, cans, never anything bought, never a doll . . . the thing was to make believe. I always wanted to have a real doll. It was a dream! And on this day, a man approached, an adult. He came close and began to talk with me. I must have been three years old but I remember everything . . . *everything*. He said that he had a doll for me in his house, a real doll. I became so happy! In my head, everything became filled with colors. I stirred with joy. It was a dream! I walked with him. When we came close to the river and no one else was nearby, he began to remove my clothes to rape me . . . and he got very close, but exactly at that moment my mother appeared!

I was there! I remember everything that happened . . . and it was the same period that she was writing her diary for Audálio. She said that she received various pieces of advice from spirits—"Vera is in danger! Vera is in danger!" She left the visitors in the shack and ran to find me. Only this didn't get into the book . . . it was never published in her diary. Audálio read and made his choices. He took out what he couldn't publish but he fulfilled his promise to find a publisher for the book. My mother had every confidence in the world in Audálio. She only spoke well of the "reporter": how he was proper, a hard worker, honest. And on the day the book was published, he was at the publisher [Francisco Alves] greeting the guests and introducing them to my mother.

The book signing was a surprise. There were so many people there when we arrived at the entrance to the bookstore . . . so many people you couldn't believe it. We were wearing new, clean clothes, new shoes. When we entered, the autograph room was already set up, with a table and chair for my mother to sit at. The invited guests were coming in— only elegant people—and standing in line to get her autograph. Some remained standing in line a very long time, until their turn came. When it was over, we were driven back to the favela by car! Every one was happy. We dined at a restaurant, we were driven around some more, we drank as many sodas as we wanted. What a delicious moment! It was an unforgettable night.

We passed suddenly from water to wine. The first months were wonderful: we slept, awakened happy, smiling. Now that my mother had received a small amount of money from the publisher, she didn't have to work any more. We almost forgot that the favela existed. We slept there, but the mess with the neighbors, the fights during the day, all were in the past. Now was our time to enjoy ourselves, to take walks, to have ice cream. In the street, people asked her for her autograph, they chatted with her, commented on the book. If you let her, she'd forget everything and stand talking in the street. When someone invited my mother for lunch in a restaurant, my brothers and I would sit quietly at the side. She found even restaurant manners strange. The places were so pretty: nice chairs, shiny knives and forks, everything pretty, clean, and different . . . even more so when the food arrived! A plate filled with food, smelling so good. I don't know if she sat staring at it or whether she stuffed her mouth quickly.

We also went from store to store to buy new clothing. There was so much selection that it was difficult to choose. I got shoes, a patterned skirt; my brothers got soccer shoes, a ball . . . everything that we always wanted to have. My mother bought beautiful clothing for herself, and perfume, cosmetics. You had to dress this way when you visited famous people. In the favela, though, things weren't good. People envied us and were humiliated to see my mother the center of such attention. Where could we move? We had no money for a real house and Audálio forgot to get us out of Canindé. The favelados got money together to buy the book, to see if someone's name they knew was in it. They didn't know how to read very well, so just seeing a name was enough to launch an accusation at my mother. When we visited a man my mother knew and she told him about conditions in the favela, he was incredulous. He said that we could move into a small, unoccupied apartment at the back of his house. It was so dark it looked like a cellar. It was much more comfortable, though, than our junk-filled shack. It really was a place to live. My mother arranged the date for our move, and on that day a truck came to pick us up. When the truck pulled up close to our shack and we started carrying our things outside, our favela neighbors began to come near. They were yelling, cursing at us. I will never forget that moving day. As we were leaving, they started throwing stones at the truck. Yes, stones!

With the money the publisher [Francisco Alves] deposited for my mother, Audálio bought a brick house for us. It was a mansion for someone from the favela. with running water, a refrigerator . . . rich things! Even more delicious was the neighborhood: Santana, an upper-class district. The sidewalks seemed to shine with cleanliness. There were big houses there, the families of important people, new cars. I even remember the school we attended. The students were clean and wore new shoes. They brought lunches from home . . . [there were] chairs, pencils, chalk, erasers. The beginning was a dream but after a few months the four of us were truly fishes out of water. The house felt to us like a prison! The neighbors blamed us for things and complained. In the favela it was easier. No one bothered about the poverty of the others. In Santana we learned about prejudice, especially the boys.

João and Zé Carlos didn't travel with my mother and me. Rather, they stayed alone at home. They used to play soccer in the street, going to the movies and returning late, but the neighborhood boys didn't do this. My brothers knew how to fly kites, to ride skateboards. Staying in the house for them was the worst thing possible. The mothers of the other boys in the neighborhood didn't want their sons to be around them. They prohibited it! The two boys were skinny, they wore hand-me-downs and looked like hoodlums . . . it was difficult to adjust. We lived there three years. Three years! My mother wrote a second diary that was published, *Casa de Alvenaria*, or House of Bricks. She explained our difficulties in adjusting, the problems she had started to have with Audálio, what she thought of rich people. People must not have liked this. They considered her indelibly marked by the favela. For example, if we went to a restaurant with someone famous, at the end of the meal my mother asked the waiter to wrap up what was left to take home. For her, throwing away food was the worst sin a poor person could commit. My mother couldn't stand seeing a beggar in the street asking for money, cold, in the rain. She didn't accept that. The rich people didn't understand this. They didn't know what is was to be cold and wet. They go to restaurants, ask for lots of food, and throw out what they don't eat. If someone in the street was having trouble, she would stop everything to take that poor person into our house . . . our house! My mother took everyone in. The result was that the neighbors complained, and the reporters wrote about it in the papers. In Santana we didn't have peace. The house was filling up with beggars. The police and the reporters didn't leave us in peace. My brothers were often separated from my mother because of her trips. In the favela we had always stayed together. This was weakening our sense of being a family. My mother became more impatient. Now she never had privacy. Even on Sundays people would come asking for help: a job, a truck, food, a bus ticket, get a relative out of jail, asking her to do everything. People came from far away . . . very far away! They arrived in the early morning and lined up to ask for things. She became known as the "Favela Queen." Audálio couldn't stand her extravagances and complained with reason. She was spending our money on others. If she had it, my mother spent it.

My mother came to regret publishing her diary. It had become impossible to deal with the lack of calm, lack of privacy, lack of respect. It seemed that everyone wanted to carve out a piece of Carolina—newspaper reporters, politicians—to use and then discard her back into misery. Even today I don't feel comfortable giving interviews: what if it's another exploiter? My mother believed in people. She was naive and believed in everybody. . . . Good memories of Santana? Yes, I have a few. Of being able to leave the violence of Canindé, of being able to travel, to visit different places, to go by airplane. More than anything it was marvelous to have breakfast, lunch, and dinner every day of the week. Food was plentiful in the house, and when my mother was invited for an autograph session . . . it was a feast! We would be put up in a pretty hotel and be invited to dinner. They always did this.

We traveled to most of the Brazilian states and to various Latin American countries. Always the two of us and Audálio. I was able to experience the sea, climb Pão de Açucar [in Rio] by cable car, and visit many other places. The book gave us a chance to realize all of the dreams we had in the favela—Carnival balls, for example. My mother loved Carnival! And with the money from the diary she ordered the most beautiful costumes for the parade. One of them, that I liked the most, was covered with spangles, all glossy and shining! My mother also wanted to sing in public, to be an actress. She did whatever she could to achieve this. She never sang over the air but she did record a samba record. It was just like her diary. She put her writing to music in verse form. A friend wrote the melody and it was ready. I still have the tape, but the record disappeared from the stores. The record contributed to Audálio and my mother's estrangement. Audálio didn't want her to make the record or anything. He just wanted her to write and to talk about her work. A life just of this would have been disagreeable, especially for my mother.

Audálio was right to a certain degree when he said that she had a difficult personality. She did, indeed. When she made a decision, it was made, period. That was it. This is why she was what she was: "the writer Carolina Maria de Jesus," as it says on her tombstone. If she hadn't been so headstrong, if she had been less willful, do you think she would have made it out of the favela? Life there was so hard, not even the men can bear it. My mother took care of her children alone, she cleaned the house, she gathered paper to sell, she cooked, she sewed our clothing. We didn't live better than the other favela families. If it hadn't been for her personality, the story would have been different. Not just any woman could have done what she did.

Audálio was one of the few persons whom my mother trusted. If he said he would do something, she didn't doubt it. He took care of our money, the trips, the public appearances. I also like Audálio, and you know that my mother's ferocity wasn't an easy thing to deal with. It wasn't everyone who could put up with her: my mother was *stubborn!* Yet if there was something she couldn't stand, it was to be controlled by others.

She wanted to control her own future, and Audálio couldn't understand this. Thus they broke up.

Audálio also doesn't admit that she was taken advantage of. Ah, was she! My mother may have not paid attention to money. I admit this. But if you examine all of the things she did—her books, the ones published in new editions, the translations—if someone looks into it, the truth will come out about the number of people who took advantage of her. Audálio, today, says that I don't know about any of this. He's talking about the time when I was a child and didn't understand things. Ridiculous! I remember. I remember many things! We lived together! At home, in hotels, on trips . . . I attended all of her talks sitting in the first row. Wherever she went, she took me with her. I virtually never played in the street because of this. Does Audálio say anything about these things, like how I accompanied her closely and knew her life from the favela to Parelheiros, where she died? And if I say that she was taken advantage of . . . that many people profited from her work, it's because I know what happened. I was over ten years of age and I wasn't deaf, nor blind.

Who has the rights for the books translated abroad? Where are they? No one knows! Her published diary was one of the most translated books in Brazilian history, even into Japanese and Russian. We've only received money from the United States[1], and I can't even be sure if what I receive from there is correct. Not a cent ever came from any of the other translations, neither when my mother was alive nor now. The problem is that my mother signed many papers. So many that it was impossible to read all of them. Now I don't know what to do because no one helps us in our life. When I ask where these papers are, or why the foreign royalties don't come, I only get excuses . . . excuses, cancelled appointments, "we'll talk about this some other time," "I'm busy now," "go talk with so-and-so." Pure evasion, and I know it . . . I know this very well!

Do you know how we bought the property in Parelheiros? Do you know why we left the "mansion" in Santana to live so far away? We paid for the land with the first part of the royalty for the film rights. An Italian production company wanted to make a film from the diary and paid, in advance, the first part of the author's rights. My mother, then, had one of her crazy ideas and decided to send Zé Carlos and me to Italy—Italy!—to play ourselves. She took money out of the advance for the plane fares, the hotels, food, and we even held reservations. João grew up quickly, and he couldn't have been able to play the part of a child even though he was the most timid of the three of us. Everything was ready—bags packed, new clothing. We could see Italy. We were all excited. A few days before our departure, my mother went to the offices of the magazine O *Cruzeiro* to resolve some contract problems and had a premonition: "They're talking about me. They want to trick me." And she was right! My brothers and I were there to confirm that it was true. She stood at the door listening carefully, quietly, and heard. Inside the room, they were talking about the royalty arrangements, and they said that my mother had received enough already . . . and that she would end up wasting it, throwing it away. This was the justification. She left without ceremony. She cancelled the flight and everything else. She took what was left and bought the Parelheiros property. Within a week we moved there.

The big difference between me and my brothers in Parelheiros was that my horizons expanded, opening new paths for my life. They, on the contrary, left behind their circle of friends. They had to change schools, to adapt to a new life away from the city. There is no doubt that we all won more freedom in our new home. We studied, worked, and defined our character as adults. João and Zé Carlos, formerly submissive to our mother, became quarrelsome with her, without fear. At times I became terrified when an argument became too heated. Zé Carlos, the most sociable, clashed less often with her because he almost never slept at home. João was more difficult. He didn't get along with strangers, he lived in the house, and I never saw him with a girl. He was considerably more timid than Zé Carlos but, as the older brother, he competed for attention from my mother. The two of them, in Parelheiros, fought like husband and wife. João came to want to decide what was best for us and my mother, intransigent, ignored him. Each one got on the other's nerves; it was a horror.

In Parelheiros, João lost his health and would have died even sooner if it hadn't been for a special medicine she made. He arrived from Santana with bad habits: he ate a good deal of junk, the kind rich people eat. In Parelheiros life was different. Food was simpler: beans, squash . . . so, as he didn't like these things, he ate in bars throughout the day and at home only drank coffee. When we didn't have sugar on Sundays (when the stores were closed), he would become irritable, searching through the entire house, under the furniture. Once he found some, a sack lost during the move from Santana. It must have been two years old or more, but João didn't care. He made coffee and filled it with sugar. My mother warned him but he didn't listen . . . an hour later he was so sick that we couldn't do anything about it. We couldn't get medical help. None of us had a work card, and the INPS [social service] hospitals required you to have one. João had a job but he had no documents, nothing. He remained very sick for three days; he could only take water. Zé Carlos and I lost hope, but my mother went into the forest on her own. She brought back a green pineapple and made a tea with the peel. João drank it and recovered, but their relationship remained bad.

Zé Carlos was my mother's favorite. He learned English, he read newspapers, magazines, books. He was super-intelligent! Everyone admired him, and when he told stories, people forgot to look at their watches. Because of this, my mother never cared if he went to work or stayed asleep. She liked Zé because he knew how to speak so well. The politicians we met praised his sharpness, his eloquence. Today people say that he never uses his intelligence. My mother is to blame. She spoiled him too much as a child. He ended up the loser. He has no goals for his life, no steady work, he lives in the street. Zé Carlos is impossible!

My mother didn't want any of to have to work like her, sacrificing her life to give comfort to others. In Parelheiros, if we didn't have food and our stomachs growled from hunger, she would disappear into the woods . . . not from the road but into the trees, sometimes for a week or more, and she always would bring back something to eat. Always. We stayed alone in our house, eating from the floor until she returned. Some people said that she was a spirit, and I agree with the possibility. She walked in the woods, slept on the ground under trees, and sometimes ended up in the city. She wasn't afraid of anything and never fell sick. She found plants, roots, and knew how to make foods and medicine completely different from the conventional menu.

My mother adored her *sítio* [country place]. If she wasn't reading, she would work in the garden. She showed such affection for the place that you can't imagine. She would say: "This is mine. Here is where I want to die, in peace." During this time, João helped at the *sítio* and worked for a firm during the day. Someone had to provide income for food, soap. The manioc we harvested wasn't enough. I began to study at night and got a job as a secretary. Zé Carlos, when he was in a good mood and

needed money, would go out and get some pick-up jobs, nothing permanent. His life never has been stable . . . even today, when he is broke, he
comes and knocks on my door. João was the opposite. He awoke at dawn
during weekdays and worked in the garden until 8:00 A.M., then went off
to work. He'd pay the bills, buy food on the way home, and when he got
back he would fix whatever needed repairs, perhaps a loose shingle, a
door hinge. His pleasure was to stay with the family. Our life was never
easy, even when we began to go to work. As the youngest, I ended up
having two jobs on top of my studies . . . an infernal schedule, going to
sleep late and awaking very early. I sped through my lunch, ate little and
slept less. My only day of rest was Sunday. Parelheiros was important for
me. There I began to study, to work, to learn to have my own life. It was
there that I met my husband, Paulo, and it also was the only place where,
in spite of everything, my mother had a little peace. For these reasons,
today I insist on saying that the *sítio* is all mine. I bought Zé Carlos's portion
and slowly have improved things. I bought a fence, lighting . . . it has
become a jewel! Today I pay someone to take care of it during the week, and
on weekends and holidays my family goes there. I'm proud of this.

At the point that each of us started to earn money, my mother was able
to work less. We would bring home food, so that she now only cooked
and, from time to time, did garden planting. She preferred to spend her
time reading and writing. She would pick me up after school at night and
we would talk about the day's lessons as we returned home. She was
interested, and learned rapidly. In a short number of years, my mother
ended up learning a good deal, both through me and on her own. Her
Portuguese style improved significantly in comparison to her early writing. I actually heard from her mouth that she was ashamed of all of the
grammatical errors in *Quarto de Despejo*, her first book. In Parelheiros
she even read encyclopedias.

My Canindé experience makes me remember things that would better
not have happened. I insist that my children understand this: the educa-
tional things that they have—school, books, travel—are so that they never
will have to experience what a favela is. The last great sadness of my life
was the death of my brother João. Exactly at a time when our lives seemed
to be improving, João and my mother died, four months apart. This was
not fair. He worked uncomplainingly. He did whatever he could to improve the quality of my mother's life. It was he who paid for her medi-

cine. If we needed to pay bills, he would work overtime. He worked day and night, weekends, holidays. And when he finished, he stayed at home with my mother. In this way they were alike; they preferred solitude to noise and commotion.

Before entering the army, João saved some money and constructed a storefront for my mother. The idea was to have something for her to do to give her tranquility in her old age. He bought a nice stock of merchandise, enough for several months. The business proved a burden because my mother sometimes forgot to charge her customers . . . she offered credit and then forgot what was owed. Then João, on top of his jobs, had to take over the store as well, until he had to enter military service. When João returned, Zé Carlos had married and moved back in with my mother. My mother hated Zé Carlos's wife. The two spent the day inside the house, drinking, doing nothing. My mother couldn't stand it, nor could João. We began to get irritated with my mother because although she was upset at the situation she did nothing. She didn't lift a finger or force Zé Carlos to shape up. João lost his patience and left. Leaving home was a torment for him. His health was already weak. Then I went to help my brother. He was doing alright, living in a rented room. After a time, though, we learned that my mother was nearly starving. João returned home and ordered Zé and his wife to pack up and leave, within three days . . . even if my mother didn't care if they stayed or not.

João had nothing to do with Zé Carlos. As long as he lived at home, we never lacked anything. He would fill the refrigerator every week with fish, ham, apples, grapes, sweets . . . whatever my mother liked, we had, but the two hardly talked to each other. Before going to work, he would do *everything*. The money he earned working went into the house. It's difficult to say if she was happier with João or living with strife with Zé Carlos, who although he caused a good deal of trouble, got along with her very well on a certain level. My mother adored him. Their conversations, the stories he told to her—João never was much of a reader, nor was he good in conversation—were more important for my mother.

The problem was Zé Carlos's willingness to take advantage of her. By this time, he already had a daughter. Because of this, he softened—and he also managed to convince her that if she helped them for a little while, things would get better. My mother, of course, didn't think twice. Within a week none of her money was left. João became suspicious: she ate almost nothing. João couldn't take it. He left for good. His illness worsened considerably after he left. He couldn't hold down any solid food. His diet was liquids and medicine. [After he was called to military service] he obtained all of his documents (his work permit, his identity card, proof of payment of taxes), and then it was easy to get him into the hospital when things worsened.

In 1976 from one hour to the next it looked as if things would improve significantly. A publisher [Edibolso of São Paulo] decided to issue a pocket-sized edition of *Quarto de Despejo*. They negotiated a contract with Francisco Alves and arranged for my mother to autograph copies of her book in various places in the city. She was delighted, naturally. It was a great success. Everywhere she appeared, people made long lines. The publisher placed placards and advertising posters in public places. She started to be invited for appearances again: [television] programs, interviews in *Manchete* magazine. At the same time, she received confirmation that Americans would be making a film about her diary. They even sent her . . . air tickets for her to watch the film being made [in Rio]. Zé Carlos helped her communicate. At that time my house hadn't been finished yet. She came to me and said that she would pay for the work to be completed. When the time came to go to Rio, she didn't have the right clothes to wear: she had no shoes, no bags, nothing. I sent her to a store to buy what she needed, to buy a decent skirt so she wouldn't be ashamed in public. I used the money I had set aside to finish my house and I paid for a temporary one to be built for Zé Carlos. I was left without a cent in my pocket. Then things crashed. I thought that things were getting better—what had to be done was to improvise—and I even took my wedding clothes and lent them to my mother for her to use. The trip was at the end of the year. She got dressed, took the airplane, spent a week in Rio and came back. On her arrival she went to Zé Carlos's house and gave his wife my dress . . . my dress . . . my wedding dress! Can things like this happen? When she came to talk to me, I became so angry that I demanded that she retrieve the dress the same day and bring it back to me. She got it, and it was the last time we saw each other.

I even remember having said that João was no better in order to see if she would come to have lunch with me the next day. A friend had invited her for a lunch especially for her. No one expected that she would die so suddenly. They say that it was a respiratory attack, but a day earlier—

one day before—she was normal, healthy, determined. Besides this, I never knew that she had bronchitis. By what they told me, she was in Zé Carlos's house when she had the attack. She couldn't breathe. The neighbor, who had a car, took all day to get dressed, but she was still alive in the car. She died on the way to the hospital. I asked that they do an autopsy on her body, it was so sudden. But only the oldest child can make this request, and it was never done. João had lost his motivation for living when he learned she had died. In the car, before dying, the last message my mother left for me was for me to take care of João. Not very many people understood their relationship: the two were obstinate to the roots of their souls, they argued about everything, but in spite of everything they were really close.

Dona Mariazinha, my mother's best friend in Parelheiros, helped us to pay for the casket, the wake, and the funeral. We were unable to obtain a place at the Vila Cipó cemetery, where she wanted to be buried. Television stations wanted to cover the funeral but they didn't know where it would be. We had no plot, nothing, but when we said that her dream was to be buried there, the city turned a deaf ear. The mayor donated a monument stone. The grave became a public site. They erected a platform and several people spoke about her, about her life, paying tribute to her. What most moved me was when the priest who was celebrating the mass, in the middle of the ceremony, said: "It is incredible that the writer Carolina Maria de Jesus is going to be buried without a single flower on her grave." At that moment, the people left the chapel—everyone at once—and ran to the gardens on the grounds of the church and cut flowers to carry to the cemetery. This was unforgettable for me. There were so many flowers that I thought: "this is what she dreamed of when she thought of her death . . . it was so beautiful, she must be happy now."

After my mother's death, João suddenly fell sick again. He spent day and night in treatment, taking blood transfusions and blood dialysis once a week. He tried every remedy possible. I called the physician and told him that he was the son of the writer Carolina Maria de Jesus, and gave him a copy of *Quarto de Despejo*. I looked up my mother's friends: Sr. Hernani, Jacinto Figueira. Dr. Zerbini, the cardiologist, said that if it were anything to do with the heart, he and his team would operate without charge. João needed a new kidney. We found a donor and arranged for an operation. A week before it was scheduled, we visited my brother in the hospital. He was very weak . . . his breathing was labored and he remained virtually immobile in bed. When I asked him what was the matter, he said to me: "Vera, mother is here. I saw mother." I was astonished by this. Mother? Three days after he received the kidney, he died. My daughter was ready to be born, and I lost my brother. For this I say: when it has to happen, there's nothing you can do. It was this way for my mother and for João as well. After my mother died, nothing changed very much. I finished my high school and my teacher training. My dreams were fulfilled: I could now teach and provide for my family. Besides, I have worked on all of the projects involving my mother's memory. She was an unforgettable person. In the future I hope to graduate from the university, to finish so I can raise my children and publicize my mother's work."

José (Zé) Carlos de Jesus, b. São Paulo, August 6, 1950. Interviewed in Benê's bar, Interlagos, São Paulo, June 27, 1992, and other locations on other dates.

I'm the second son of Carolina Maria de Jesus, the child in the middle. It isn't much, but they say that I seem older than men of my age. I was born in São Paulo. From the hospital I went directly to the favela named Canindé. I spent my infancy there, through adolescence. I left in the 1960s, when my mother's talent was recognized through her greatest publishing success, *Quarto de Despejo*. We spent several years in Santana, in a brick house, but things soured, and we moved to a rural plot in Parelheiros, on the southern periphery of the city of São Paulo. Although I lived in Santana, I think the favela is in my blood, as it was in my mother's.

I remember her very well. The two of us used to talk a lot . . . really a lot! We used to talk about everything under the sun. It was unbelievable, but it seemed like we used to think the same way and we liked the same things. From the time that I was a baby until she died, the old lady and I had that kind of relationship, based on mutual understanding. We used to talk about everything: religion, psychology, science, everything. There was no limit to knowledge as far as we were concerned. We loved politics the most . . . Brazilian politics. We used to spend nights talking about it, and some nights we didn't even go to bed because we talked so long. We were the most revolutionary in our family, the most restless. My mother's dream was always to come to São Paulo. She wanted to work, to improve her life and get better health treatment for her mother. Apparently her

Zé Carlos de Jesus. Photograph by Juliano Spyer.

stepfather wouldn't let them leave Minas. And my mother, because of
that, hated Minas Gerais to the day she died. Prejudice, misery, racism,
she hated all of that.

In my case it's no different. I'm known in these parts as one of the best
truckers in São Paulo. Trucking is the only profession that works for me.
I'm sort of a lone wolf, I just want to stay far away . . . far away. On the
road nobody bothers me. I don't have to explain myself or apologize. I
travel around and get to know the country, the reality and misery of Brazil.
I learned to love misery like my mother did. This is a miserable country
and if you don't get to know the poverty and the garbage, you won't have
learned anything about it—not a thing. Carolina was like that and she
died because of that philosophy of ours. What she saw in the slums no
one else noticed . . . the politicians who showed up during election time
and even took rotten food to give to the people, she reported everything
. . . until she got tired.

Basically, the difference between me and my mother is that she was

naive. She confronted the system, challenging people who were too powerful. She was a favelada who wanted to be a writer. She complained,
rubbed salt into the wounds of the biggest political caciques, and ended
up not understood, almost as miserable as when she was in Canindé. I
learned this lesson from her: stand at a distance from fame and recognition. Where did her heroism get her, I ask? While the intellectuals write
theses about poverty, she, semi-literate, wrote a book that touched multi-
tudes . . . the greatest publishing success of the day! Where did it get her?
Today she's dead, buried, and vanished from Brazilian memory.

The word was her only weapon. "The favelada with the fiery tongue"
is how politicians referred to my mother. She would attend political
speeches during elections to scavenge for electoral posters and leaflets,
but she became excited at what she heard. The security guards were warned
not to interfere with the black lady and they always let her go up on the
speakers' stand. She'd go up on the stand and beat up anyone, even
Adhemar de Barros. She respected Adhemar, but she lacked the right touch.
She was too powerless to confront the big shots.

In Argentina, they say that people like my mother have a "screw loose."
So the Argentinians presented her with a large metal screw. It was for her
to replace the one she had missing. Do you think it did any good? Carolina once, Carolina always the same. That's what I say. And worse all the
time! Every artist is just like her, and it has to be like that, it has to be like
that to have freedom. Carolina Maria de Jesus was born to be a writer,
whether poor or rich. Her expressive powers, her poetry, came from her
spirit. One example I remember by heart: "Do you know what color
Brazil is? Brazil's is gray and its sky is yellow." This was what she told a
reporter from *Pravda* about Brazil's problems. What a beautiful answer!
She said that to explain what hunger felt like: you only get yellow and
gray from hunger, after going four days without eating.

In Canindé, thanks to my mother's uncommon effort to keep us from
dying of hunger, I survived. I had a regular childhood, just like any other
slum kid in São Paulo. At that time, the old favelas were miserable but
there was solidarity among its residents. They were not as violent or as
marginal as they are today. In Canindé, if someone got sick, the neighbors would go to our shack to lend money, and they even loaned money
to buy medicine. My mom was like that, too. This was the great difference. Carolina, my mom, acted like a security guard in the favela. If there

were fights in the middle of the night, a man beating his wife, she would send my brother João to take care of us and then leave to call the police. She would file a complaint and file the papers. The slums used to be like that: one needs something and the other helps, understand? I think that thirty years ago there was a lot more solidarity among the poor than among the rich.

Life was healthier in the favelas in those days. Boy, was it! We'd go to school, have a snack in the afternoon, and then come back. My friends and I would go out to "run the market" [*correr feira*]. Don't you know what that is? This was what all the little slum kids did, grabbing fruit on the sly, stealing sweets, and, on top of everything, earning tips by carrying packages. We'd build a little car out of a box and ball bearings to carry the groceries or we'd pick up boards and leftovers to sell later. We'd end up spending the day out of the house. My mom would be picking up refuse with Vera on her back and João and I would take off around here. Everything would end up in a soccer game, naturally.

What I liked least was going to school. They did have good quality public schools with competent teachers, but people who lived in the slums suffered all kinds of prejudice when they went to school. Children played without danger, more jobs were available, you could feed your children better. Society discriminated against slum people much more in the 1950s. Walking into a bank, a store, even a school was more difficult. You had to have money, because appearance was paramount in those places. On the other hand, poor people were not feared, as they are today. Any ragged kid in the street is seen as a thief. We were mischievous, not criminals. We represented no threat to society. People gave charity for the less fortunate without being afraid, and an unemployed father was respected by upper class people. We made the rounds of houses asking for food, but it wasn't just food they would give us. No! They'd give food, clothes, an old bicycle, used toys. I never heard of people talking about kids who stole, just a little fruit, not very much, just kid things. And people who lived in the slums weren't as poor as they are now. There was a friend of mine who died not long ago who was a lawyer and who had lived in a favela. There were lawyers in the favelas! Favelados took university courses at night and worked during the day, as several of my friends did.

Because of this I believe that *Quarto de Despejo* today is a book that is more and more relevant. I wish it weren't, but it is! It would be better if

things had been different, but Brazil preferred silencing my mother's message to opening its eyes. Now what we see out of the window is a sea of
garbage—misery on the outskirts of the cities, misery on the bus, misery
downtown, misery, misery, misery! I know that our country doesn't like
to advertise its poverty and misery. No country does. It exists in the U.S.,
but it is more hidden. The proof is that my mother's book sells there.
Brazilian popular culture acknowledges poverty. Popular music and art is
about poverty. Here, the people protest by singing about our disgrace.

I've read everything she wrote. When her diary first came out, there in
the slum they only bought one. No one had any money, but they took up
a collection and bought one and passed it around. I lived through all that,
man. Vera wasn't very old, she didn't know much about it. I read and
lived everything my mother wrote! And the book of hers I loved the most
was *Diary of Bitita*. That's a book I'd really like to push to make it better
known. It didn't have the encouragement it deserved. Not at all.

My old lady was like that. She'd really give it to 'em. In her book *Casa
de Alvenaria* she wrote a poem about the colonists and the plantation
owners, a denunciation, pure and simple, from start to finish. She wrote
about the reason for rural flight, the exodus from rural areas, the exploitation. She felt it was absurd for anyone to go hungry in the middle of a
plantation. And I think so too! How can that be? Planting, harvesting,
and dying from hunger. My mother was one of the biggest fans of Carnival I ever knew. The five days of Carnival were sacred for her. She danced
a great samba . . . the swarming streets, the hot music, and Carolina
dancing! Every year she dressed in her costume of spotted Carijó chicken
feathers, and danced until the sun came up. She composed Carnival songs,
sang, danced. Her love for samba was so great that right after publishing
her diary she set it to verse, transforming Canindé's sad stories into the
upbeat melodies of samba.

My mother was wild. She wouldn't run away from a fight. There were
bearded men in the favela who were afraid of my old lady. And the worst
way to upset her was to mess with us kids. We only had her and she only
had us, so that was our treasure. If anyone provoked her kids or laid a
hand on them, they were sorry afterwards. Without her we would have
died. And we gave her back that attention. We stuck to her like glue. My
mom was father and mother. She got in the middle of a knife fight once to
protect my brother. He was messing around with some prostitutes in the

favela. I think he told one of them off and then ran away. The woman was furious and came after him with a knife. He was about six years old. When the prostitute pulled out the knife, my mom jumped on her. She was going to save João any way she could, at any cost, and she ended up getting stabbed five times. The prostitute was going to kill him . . . put a hole right through him. My mother was going to die for my brother if necessary.

She ended up staying in the hospital for three months. During that time we had to make do all by ourselves. It was tough! My sister was only three and João was the one who supported us. He'd go out hunting for food and I had to stay with her in the shack. And I couldn't even go out because the prostitute's girl friends wanted to get us, too. We spent three months without seeing the old lady and I didn't even know if she had died or not. We stayed by ourselves until the social service came and took my brother and sister and me away. As a matter of fact, Vera's godmother is the same social worker who took us away from the slum, Marta Terezinha Godinho. She lived near the favela and knew my mom quite well. The two were friends. She took us to the house of a lady she knew and we stayed there until my mother got well.

My mother was dogmatic. She was always a fighter in a war that never let up! Like Zumbí of Palmares [the military leader of a 17th-century community of escaped slaves], her haughtiness was evidence of her inheritance of African nobility . . . an Amazon . . . an African queen bee, protecting her family and her hive with every bit of strength she had. She was this way with her children and before that, with her mother. In school she was the only black child in the class. School was for whites only and she was someone who wanted to study, she enjoyed that, okay? She read a lot because she couldn't go to school. She only finished the second grade. Black students only went through the second grade . . . there was no third or fourth grade, it was just to learn to read and that was it. Reading . . . was just to help sell some fruit, make out some bills and that was it. That was enough. I just know that she ended up providing for everyone, her mother, her stepfather, her brother. She was the one who steadied the helm for everyone.

Here in São Paulo things weren't easy. Contrary to what one heard in the countryside, São Paulo wasn't the eighth wonder of the world. It was hard to earn a living, but despite her jobs, my mother continued to read and to write. She published some things in newspapers. She wrote poems, fragments of plays, novels, a little of everything. From the time my mother was a small girl she was always against that kind of exploitation, against all that brown-nosing. She really looked up to someone who was good, not just anyone or just because they were white. You don't need to be white or black to be good. At that time everyone thought that white was good and black was bad. Carolina thought differently: white and black, if they were good for nothing they were all the same. And that's why she really gave it to them. She'd cuss plantation owners, judges, lawyers, whoever it might be. Even with her family she was always having knock-down, drag-out fights! She's the one who was supporting everyone and she'd still get beatings.

If a circus came, right away she went to the director and offered to be in it. She designed her own costumes. She sang a lot in a circus called Xororó before we were born. She had one costume all made of feathers, and another full of lights. My mom was a very good singer, even more so with those exotic costumes, I think it was a fine show. The stage was completely dark and then a big black lady came out, all lit up. That was my mother! And in spite of all the difficulties, she never gave up. She was a real "bombshell" as they say in the Northeast. A bombshell and a hard bone to gnaw.

When she arrived in São Paulo she didn't just sit around. And the city didn't frighten her. Not at all. She just showed up and got a job right away. She worked as a maid for rich people, the high bourgeoisie. She wanted to work for the elite, because that way she could be next to cultured people. She enjoyed reading a lot and used to say that in a house where there's no books or culture, there's no spirit either. As a domestic, her income was assured: room and board and a salary to send home to Minas. Her employers, rich people, liked her work but especially appreciated the fact that she was different from other maids. She read newspapers, books, and could converse with anyone. My mother had a kind of high spirituality, pride, and because of this she never kowtowed to her bosses. I learned this lesson from her: poverty does not mean inferiority.

In the mansions in which she worked, her employers respected her as an equal human being, not as an ignorant nobody! My mother would never accept such treatment. But when she started to have children—one, two, three—she couldn't work any longer as a live-in domestic. She couldn't be a mother and at the same time do the work. This challenge wasn't easy. We ended up in the favela and she made the decision to scavenge for paper in the street. My mother woke up early, prepared coffee, nursed Vera, dressed everyone, and we all left for the street. Her mother had died, and, with her, her last family link to Sacramento. So she resolved to construct a hut in Canindé because at least in her free time and at night she could read books. In Canindé, except for the fights that she broke up, generally at night, the situation permitted her to have creative activity . . . her internal misery. From the favela she produced her greatest amount of work.

I think she actually got along better with rich people than with the slum dwellers. People got upset because she wrote about their lives; they didn't like that. There in the slum no one understood that *Quarto de Despejo* was a denunciation, right? She didn't write out of meanness. She wrote for the sake of writing, because she enjoyed it. So in the favela the people didn't appreciate that. They were jealous or something, I don't know. She became famous, went around in a taxi . . . or a great big car with a driver would pick us up at our door. The favelados didn't like it. They said she had taken advantage of them and the situation grew more tense by the day. There were some characters giving us dirty looks, grumbling a lot. They started to make threats, threats, until a friend came by and said: "Look, you've got to get out of here, 'cause if you don't, they could even kill you."

That week my mother called on a friend of hers, Mr. Antônio Soeiro Cabral, the manager of the Sugar Loaf food store, who had read her book. He offered for us to stay in a house of his in Osasco as long as we needed. After my mother's royalties started being deposited in the bank, Audálio bought a house for us, ex-favelados, in the "chic" district of Santana. Audálio, though, who was a journalist [and not familiar with real estate], started out doing the deal the wrong way: he bought the house with people inside, with renters living there. The woman who sold the house sold it because she couldn't get those people to leave. So when we got to the house with the moving truck my mother went up to the house and said: "Look, I'm not going to stay out here in the street because the house belongs to me." So we all ended up living together, our family and the renter's family. The truck came with all our stuff, we put everything inside and we started living with the people. It turned out that we all got along really well. My mom would fix a lamb shank, chicken and brown gravy, macaroni and we'd eat it all together. After a while they got another house and left. My mother could have evicted them, but she understood their plight; she accepted them. Favela dwellers always are willing to take in one more person.

When our new Santana neighbors saw our truck coming, they locked their doors. Why? We were intruders, dirty, we looked the way favelados look. Mothers kept their children inside so they would not get involved with "bad company." In time people realized that such worries were unfounded. In Santana, I missed Canindé. The street games were in my blood. The debris of the favela I remembered as a playground. My mother also missed some of her old friends. I got into a lot of mischief then. I used to be a rascal. I'd catch the bus, go out in the evening and not come back until early the next morning, if I came back at all. I had a lot of friends, the ones from Santana, the ones from the favela, some from school, and some from the street. There was never a lack of fun things to do. And even when we came into the money, wow, it was a ball! I'd go over to the favela and the guys would ask me: "Hey, Blacky, your mom's got a bunch of dough, right?" "That's right and I've got some change here to buy candy. . ." and it was like that every day. We had a great time! When I missed school I'd cut class to go play and when I got home my mother would give me a licking and I don't really blame her. Any mother who's a real mother worries about her kids, wants the best for them. It so happens that I was always sort of a black sheep. I didn't much like school. It was boring! I never ran away from a beating. I'd leave school knowing that I was going to catch it and I never thought my mother was wrong.

The mothers in Santana were watching us, for us to adapt. We were very creative. They were middle class but didn't have a bit of creativity. So then we got there and started spinning tops right away, playing "chula" and "pool cue," games we played in the slums, poor people's games. They had bikes, motor scooters, but their stuff wasn't all that great. They weren't all that fun. We arrived with a different proposition. Our activity was a lot healthier. That's when we busted in: "Hey, you don't know how to play "chula", Buddy? Come on, let's go play a little "chula." And they ended up playing with us all day long. The mothers, then, just went crazy! In the end they gradually got used to it, but at first, every time we'd go outside they'd say "Heaven help us." Blowing up balloons, making little cars out of ball bearings and pipes, that's a lot more fun, right? We were poor but a lot happier than the kids on the street. And to this day when I go over there they'll tell me, "Hell, Zé, it was great that you guys came to live here, if not I never would have learned how to really have fun." Can you imagine, they didn't even know how to play hooky! Even hooky, which was my specialty. And from the looks of things, you never played hooky, right? I knew it!

There's one thing about my mother I really admire. Really! Because you were honest, because you never lied, she respected you. I never lied to her. Never! She knew everything I did and she really got after me. She thought that was the right thing to do, that it was wrong otherwise, and she'd beat the hell out of me. She didn't want to change our personality. Not a bit! For her, it didn't matter if one son was an engineer and the other fixed umbrellas. Everyone was a person and I admire that deeply. She had an image, she was intellectual, wrote books, she was famous but she never tried to get us to be what *she* wanted. Each of us was the way we were, as long as we were honest, of course.

In Santana, we lost the down-to-earth contact we had with other people in the favela. We exchanged this for a more comfortable life, but it wasn't good. Until we got to Parelheiros, we had never worked before. She never would let us. When she bought her place, we took care of it for her. We could work only if it was for her. If the situation got tight, we suffered! We really suffered! We would plant, plant, plant some more, and nothing. What could we do? João and I had to find some outside job. If not, we just wouldn't make it, understand? We'd starve to death if she didn't let us help out. In the beginning we'd lie about it. Little fibs, you know. I'm going to visit a friend, and I'd go out and shine shoes. The other said he had to stay after school to do some makeup work and he'd go around selling fruit. Afterwards she got used to it. We grew some and had more freedom, but before that the only way we could do anything on our own was by tricking the old lady.

Besides that, we had to study and pass to the next grade. My mother was a master sergeant. She'd wake up early, fix breakfast, call her children, and she was already working. We'd spend the whole day in the country. We planted potatoes, corn, manioc, everything. I did that nonstop and João and Vera, too. That sister of mine was a firebrand. Just like her mother, she never shied away from work. She's strong today because she yanked out so many tree stumps. She'd yank and pull, clear the forest and plant. And afterwards, no time to rest. We still had to go to school in the evening. It was a tough haul.

Now just see how my mother was right. Vera's married, she has four children plus a daughter of mine she's taking care of. She's studying literature at the university. She works, she's a teacher in two schools. She's a warrior, like her mom. Teacher, student, mother. She took after her mother, no doubt about it. And she was always like that. She always worked all day long to help out at home, like my mom. She studied on her own. If they found a book in the garbage they'd pick it up and bring it home. And besides that, they'd spend the night reading and they didn't rest until they finished the book.

My mother said that her diary wasn't a good book, that it was ugly, too hard, and she never liked it. My mother could have written more, much more! And better works than her first books. No one wanted to publish novels, which is what she liked to write. You see the way Brazil is. No one ever supported her in the novel, and she became disillusioned. She ended up going back to poverty. To forget that she went away and forgot about fame. People wanted her to keep writing gossip, talking about other people's lives. My mother said no to those people. She didn't want to hear anymore about writing a diary. She wanted to be known for her novels. The articles my mother liked, or the ones she had written were all kept in a box. She kept poetry, articles, short stories.

My mother admired honesty, you understand. And in Brazil it doesn't do any good to be serious like her. An honest person, hard working . . . it doesn't do any good! The man she admired the most was her grandfather. And she admired the old guy because he was honest. She was always talking about him, always. She was always quoting stuff he had told her. The homilies and the stories also. And that's the reason she was a person who trusted others. And if a person trusts you then you have to be reliable too. If someone [played a trick] on my mother she'd get upset, feel hurt. She didn't know how to play a dirty trick to get even. She didn't know how. Well, she maybe knew how but she couldn't do it. That's why they slipped her in the middle of those politicians and she was too hot to handle. She noticed everything, everything that was going on. If anyone pulled a dirty trick she'd see it. Petty politics à la Adhemar. No one fooled Carolina. She'd look around and discover what was going on. That's why they'd slip her in the middle of the politicians—to squeeze out the crap—but afterwards she didn't want to anymore.

My mother always wanted to put in an appearance, to show what she was thinking . . . and she said whatever she damn well thought! I always said this to her: "Mom, you always want to make an appearance, right?" and she would laugh. It's true, though! If a circus came by . . . you know that Carolina was the first to show up. She'd play a little trick, she'd go talk to the owner: "Look, I've got this costume that lights up . . . I sing pretty well." Then all the favelados went to see her sing. Everyone! The circus filled up to see her doing the samba there. She used to dance a great samba, buddy! I'm telling you! A great samba. She used to compose . . . my mother has a samba LP which is pretty as hell. All artists are show-offs. A painter likes to show off so he paints his own picture and a writer writes an autobiography. It's normal, I know. It's normal for them. That's the true writer, always creating polemics. It might be with Leonel Brizola, Jângo, she didn't care. She was there in the middle making a big shebang! They were acquaintances of hers during that time, Adhemar de Barros, Jânio.[2] The ones who had their rights cancelled by the military regime, right? It was one argument after another . . . they never stopped. They would talk about the farm workers' disputes, Lenin, Getúlio Vargas. She was an excellent debater—an artist and an activist at the same time, like [the Chilean poet] Pablo Neruda. She was an activist in politics. Our life didn't change much with the book. Everything stayed about the same, a little more food, and that was it. The poor are poor, right? Even if you win the lottery, you're poor. You may have money, but at heart you're poor. My mother was poor economically when she was in Canindé but she never lacked moral values. She had a notion of what was right and what was wrong, and with this sense she'd talk to politicians and discuss with them the community's problems, right inside the favela! Today when I pass near a favela I feel very sad. The children live in the streets on their own. Like I said, *Quarto de Despejo* is becoming more and more relevant.

If she had to pick up paper again, she'd go. Her spirit was that of a poor person, a paper scavenger, and that is really, really hard to change in people, their spirit. Jesus Christ was poor, but he could have been rich. It's clear that he was—a noble family, carpenter. A carpenter at that time built ships; he was an outfitter, understand. That's what I'm trying to put in front of you. You understood the viewpoint. Jesus was poor because he chose to be, and even if he had wanted to be rich, he wouldn't make it. It's predestination . . . it's in your spirit before you're born.

In order to talk about those things you've gotta have some liquor. Brazilian *pinga*! I'm a communist but I don't drink vodka. Like my mother, I'm half communist. You can talk about that now without being afraid because communism's over with, right? If not, we'd be torn apart around here. In my opinion, freedom is fundamental! My mother was poor materially, but her greatest poverty was in her soul, like any artist or revolutionary. Pablo Neruda, Ché Guevara, Picasso all had screws loose, and they knew misery. You have to seize indignation and craft it into your art. Artists can't abide suffering. They have to say what needs to be said and even sacrifice themselves, like Ché. Me? I'm no writer, but I'm not a conformist either. No way! I'm an anarchist and a socialist, that's for sure. Socialism is communism that hasn't missed the train of history because of dogmatism. And I never conform to anything that's a sure thing, that's on the right track. When everything is very right in my life, right away I'll do something to complicate the situation. If not, it's no fun any longer, right? Socialism, in Brazil, would have had a chance if it hadn't been for the corrupt politicians. Poverty here makes friends, not enemies. People stand together without fear. I want to have a good house, good food, I'm ashamed to go dirty, I create problems for others, but I never will step on anyone else to improve my own life. I refuse categorically to do this! Brazilians are naturally socialists, without having to be doctrinaire. We're a country of mendicants. The poor ask for things from the rich, the rich from foreigners, and in the end the only one who profits is the foreigner who didn't ask for anything but who lives off the interest. In Brazil, if a labor union wants to strike, they talk and talk and talk, and the workers' condition never improves.

I was always the big conversationalist in the family. I've made friends with everyone, rich, poor, middle class. I don't have any prejudices, I take people the way they are. My mother was also a great chatterbox so we got along well. Really well! I was the one who got the most beatings at home. For any little thing I'd get a spanking, but my mother was also loving toward me. She respected my freedom. I'm the craziest one of the three and she was like that, too. They even wrote an article in the paper: "Carolina: Crazy?" I think that's what it was. It had in it everything she had done, what she said, but it came out only after she died. She wasn't crazy—crazy people say things that are incoherent. Even someone who's crazy can have coherent thoughts. Like Nietzsche . . . he died crazy and he wasn't crazy. The things he said made sense. And he was a great philosopher. Hitler's favorite philosopher. I consider myself half crazy but my craziness is healthy. I don't bother anyone with my thoughts. I don't try to annoy others. I was that way in school, but I'd cut class to not bother the others. I repeated some years but I kept going up to high school. Then I got married. I got married and I had to leave school to go to work and pay the rent. Poor people these days just get worse when they go to school.

Why? It's our government. They cut back on free education . . . the government did a Portuguese number on studying, right? They took away the chance for anyone to lead a decent life while studying. Can I speak the truth? They screwed Brazil, screwed her! Today there's no opportunity to work. I met a friend the other day who's an engineer. An engineer selling cereal. Rice and beans. A hydraulic engineer working in a grocery store. A grocery store! And there's a bunch of them, not just one or two. The one who's a little better works in a bank. All of them have graduated! And we live in that shit. Shit! We don't have any other choice. From the time we were kids we've been needy. My brother and sister and I were never children . . . never had a childhood. Childhood is having a bicycle and going for a ride, going to the Playcenter. I never had a childhood. We spent our whole life running after food.

Did you ever see people starve to death? Well, I did and I saw people die while they were eating, eating rotten stuff! They died . . . poisoned. People know that the food's rotten but hunger is stronger than reason. So then the guy doesn't have any notion he can die. He doesn't have any notion about anything. At least he dies with his belly full. I just think that's the end of the road. I work with freight that goes by truck and I see the waste, you know. In a country with such abundance, like Brazil, you just can't understand why those things happen. Every time I unload a truck full of rice I throw one sack out. Imagine that, a truck that I'm unloading—you throw one sack away. One sack always [comes to pieces] when you load the truck so you have to throw it out. Now just imagine how many trucks full of rice there are just here in São Paulo. How many sacks of rice go into the garbage? That's an insult . . . it's an insult to nature itself.

I think, according to my philosophy, that no one is obliged to stay with anyone. I also think that there are a lot of ways for you to leave a person, right? I'm a sociable person, you understand. I work in transportation because I have to, but really I'm an artist. And artists have to be sociable. Just look around: Michael Jackson, John Lennon. It's your brain that counts. Your head, your thoughts, the way you talk! I'm so sociable that I was even invited to go on a trip to Japan. For nothing, with all expenses paid. The thing is that I once worked for a Japanese fellow who used to lived near Parelheiros. He lived there but in Japan he was very rich and he was going to take me there on a trip. Why didn't I go? Who knows? It's a mystery, but I just don't leave Brazil. I can't. I have everything in order to leave and I don't go. I've already gone as far as the border, but if I pass over to the other side, I'll never come back. I received an invitation to live in Mexico, and live well! At the last minute I turned it down. I sleep in the gutter and I don't leave the country. I think my brother and sister felt the same way. We needed to live near our mother. Vera could have been in any other neighborhood but no! She'd get in the car and go from her house to the farm in half an hour. João, while he was alive, also lived near her. Except they both died about the same time, in 1977.

If you were to burn all your things, there wouldn't be a spoonful of ashes left. Look at Benê[3], for example. You think that if I'm hungry I can't come and have lunch? Of course, all I have to do is say: "Benê, give me a plateful of food 'cause I didn't work today and I'm hard up." And just like that, he'll give me the plate. No problem. Either that or he'll get me some money to eat later. You can believe that a friend in the public square is better than money in your pocket. If I wanted I could be rich today. Rich as hell! In Parelheiros I worked in the daytime and studied at night. And at that time working at night was the thing to do. That's where you earned the best money and I gave it up. I preferred going to school. I sacrificed everything for knowledge. I studied at night and couldn't work. I worked as an assistant just to hold on. The Pirelli company called me to work at night and I said: "I can't because I'm studying." I'm a bunch of things but I don't do anything right. Isn't that what my sister said about me? I don't care. Let 'em talk bad, but let 'em talk! I'm also a toolmaker. Not like my sister's husband. He's had a lot more experience than I have [and is a highly-trained mechanic]. My sister wouldn't even have to work if she didn't want to. She could just stay and take care of the house and there wouldn't be any problem. She works because it's the old lady's style. Her husband is head of a tool shop.

I don't much care for that kind of work. I respect my brother-in-law. It has nothing to do with him, but I prefer living like a nomad. People of my kind are like a steward: they do everything. They don't like to be tied down. They need a variety of things. If not, life becomes impossible. Just because of that, everyone tries to take advantage of you. Then it's easy: you get going. I've gone so far as to leave my documents in a company and take off. I can spot exploitation a long way off and I want to keep my distance, buddy. I like to have friends, to go to parties, to have fun because you only live once, friend! Working eight hours a day in a room isn't for me . . . always the same routine. I prefer to go hungry and play a game of cards with my friends, drinking a *caipirinha* [*pinga* with lime]. I'm a communist! I don't drink vodka but I love *pinga*! It's better to be a friend. When it's for a friend everything is easier. You help a friend because you enjoy it and not because you're obliged. You help a person because he deserves your friendship and because you like him.

Communism is more or less like that. I mean, not all communism but just the socialism part! That's it. That's where it's really great! I'm a socialist and I think I have the right to get a blanket from my mother and give it to my friend. That's what I think! Because he doesn't have one and my mother has four. She has four more than she needs so she gives one to me and I give it to my friend. I don't lie to her. There's no problem if I get one and tell her it's for me. I just don't do those things. No way. I'm speaking the truth: "I'm going to get one of yours and give it to my friend." It was always like that at home. If there were fifty cruzeiros on top of the fridge, I'd take them! I'd take them and not feel a bit bad about it. I wanted to play a little snooker over at the bar and that's what I'm going to say afterwards. That's how it is. My mother was always like that. What you can't do is tell a lie. The important thing is your conscience and your honesty. That's it exactly!

I went to [Parelheiros] when I was about fourteen and stayed until I got married. But it wasn't a good marriage; I didn't find one of these special ones! As they say in Zulu, I didn't find a good captain for my boat! She abandoned me in the street. She jumped ship for no reason. I don't like the kind of people who run after passions. They do a lot of stupid things and end up hurting others, and that's what happened to me.

She found someone else and left. Shall we drink one more to drown the tears? After I got married I went away to live. I bought some property and with the help of my friends I started to build. The Jesus family became quite disconnected after we grew up. We all like each other, but we can't be close by. If my sister were here we'd be at each other. Everything in a civilized way, of course. Differing points of view. And the points of view in my family are much debated. Highly debated. I reflect one way, you reflect another. That's when the argument starts. Everyone's different. Each one is [an individual]. Gradually we grew up. I learned English listening to songs and reading. I love to read! My thoughts are free. I sleep in the street. I like to read everything that shows up in my hands. Everything! Newspapers, books, anything that falls in my hands. Preferably politics! My mother controlled her children's personalities. Since we've grown up, it got hard for her to keep hold of us. João was quiet and a hard worker. I've never seen anyone enjoy working like he did. My mother would say: "We're gonna hoe weeds tomorrow," and no one complained. He'd wake up earlier than anyone else. By six in the morning he was already out weeding. My mother was a patriarchal type and she reconciled everything. She gave orders like a boss and they got done. No one answered back. There was no argument. João didn't like Parelheiros. Never did like it. My brother liked intellectual people. Only intellectuals. Because he also liked to study. He only talked with high-caliber people. He didn't pay attention to just anyone. And he was determined. So he decided to do his thing. Boy, we really liked each other but we didn't get along very well. That's the way brothers are, they love each other but they don't understand each other. If I get sick, I go to Vera's house. If I need food, she'll give it to me. When the situation gets tight we stick together, but I like to keep my distance.

I'd like to stay closer to her but we're too different. I love my nieces! I go there and they all treat me super fine. Did you see Vera's oldest son? I have the greatest esteem for that kid . . . João's spirit. Just alike, even the way they talk. He only talks about serious things. He's already an adult. When you talk with him, you'll see. You'll think you're talking to a grownup. I enjoy him. I tell him jokes, enjoy being with him. That's what life's about. You're not supposed to take things too seriously. You could go off the deep end! I grab my nephew and tell him: "Go live your life, you rascal! Your dad has money." [I make fun of him], but it's true. Sometimes we get to arguing just like adults and he really gets after me, buddy! You wouldn't believe it: "Look, uncle, don't you think the way you're going is wrong?" You need to take a look at things. I think it's neat. I tell everyone: "Take a look at João over there!" Family is family, and you just can't leave them and forget them. That's part of life, right?

I'm like a piece of wood in the river. I flow with the current. And as a matter of fact, I'm very well thought of. Hard as it is to believe. You're talking with "high shoes." My nickname here is "high shoes." You talk about high shoes around here, everyone knows who you mean. "The King of the Helpers!" I speak English really well! Recently I almost went to work for Mercedes Benz. And in that job I'd be earning more than my sister, but I turned it down. I could have even gone to Japan. I almost went to Mexico on an excellent job but I ended up deciding to stay here in Brazil. I work at lots of things: I'm an iron worker, a painter, a newspaperman, a salesman. The only thing I demand in jobs in that I keep my freedom. Without this I won't work. I do nothing! My friends are my family. They don't care if Carolina Maria de Jesus was or wasn't part of the story. Most of them don't know who the woman was. I prefer it this way: I like to express myself, to laugh. Like John Lennon, life is in the head and its ideas. Deep in my heart I'm an artist, one who wants to talk, to be creative. My marriage failed because of this spirit I have. She didn't understand me, so she found someone else and left with him. Our children stay with friends, in orphanages, and I can't help them now.

Vera is also family, only we aren't together very much. I have my ideas and she has hers. We don't agree about many things but this divergence is constructive. She is feisty, just like my mother. Everything has to be done her way. She decides something and I disagree. If this is the way she wants it, it's her life. I see no problem in us being apart . . . this is normal, it happens in many families. The tide is running against me, bringing bad luck. If there is something I should do, is to try a new direction for the life of my daughters. I'd like them, at least, to be together and to be able to go to school. Nothing more.

Carolina's strength of personality was so great that her family fell apart as soon as she died. Nonetheless, Zé Carlos and Vera, in their different ways have labored to preserve their mother's legacy. Tellingly, Vera and Zé Carlos's very different reactions to their mother's story reflect the ways that lower-class women and men are socialized in Brazil. Vera, although assertive and proud, puts honoring her mother's memory ahead of any personal bitterness towards the treatment Carolina received that Vera feels. Vera's younger brother Zé Carlos remains defiant like Carolina. He is convinced that regardless of his mother's legacy, "nothing will change the fact that we are just poor folks, and colored."

The way that both Zé Carlos and Vera remember their mother is touching. Carolina worked diligently to tell them her life story and they show gratitude to her in turn. There is no evidence in the interviews of persons close to Carolina granted to the authors of this book that Carolina ever considered herself a failure. She protected her children fiercely and they turned out well, all things considered. As a result of his being called for military service, João was the first member of the family to gain working papers, the initial step in passing from the anonymous underclass to the established working class. Because he had proper documentation, when he fell ill he was treated in a hospital. Carolina had received hospital treatment too, after she was stabbed in Canindé, but her treatment resulted from the personal intervention of the mayor. Her case, therefore, was a remnant of the old populist political style of the 1950s and remarkable confirmation that even as an indigent she was heard because of her forceful personality.

Carolina's children believe that their mother's contradictory and picaresque tendencies were engaging, not negative, aspects of her personality. When they were growing up in a perilous and impersonal environment, Carolina filled them with stories about her rural childhood in Minas Gerais and about her family. In fact, Zé Carlos claims that he remembers little else about their early conversations. More even than her fame as a writer, he recalls her maternal strength and honesty. There is a contrasting view—that Carolina and her children, because they were special, were more influenced by their favela experience than were their neighbors. "They suffered more, were hungry more often than others, but they still did not mix. The way Carolina's children were brought up was sad," Marta Teresinha Godinho commented in her interview. For Godinho, the trained social worker who worked with Carolina's family while they were in Canindé, children growing up in a favela could not be normal; the place for "normal" people, even poor ones, was outside of the favela.[4] Zé Carlos's remembers a very different childhood. Thanks to his mother's uncommon efforts to feed and protect her family, his childhood was no different from that of any poor youth in São Paulo. In her interview, Vera acknowledged that she owed everything to her mother. Everyone struggled in the favela, but the majority succeeded only in surviving, not in improving their condition. Neither Vera nor Zé Carlos deals with the certainty that had Carolina's diary not been published, they would have remained in the favela regardless of their mother's will to sacrifice.

Strangers faulted Carolina for being vain and eccentric but her children recall her talent in compensating for the limitations of their life of poverty. Vera as an adult exhibits her mother's dedication to her family, to hard work, and to striving to better herself. Her gratitude to her mother has created in her an almost sacred mission to gain recognition for her mother's achievements. She often speaks about Carolina as if she had not died twenty years ago. Zé Carlos's life, on the other hand, reflects Carolina's other side: her pride, her bohemian appetites, her fierceness, and her independence. Zé Carlos drifts through life; Vera abides strictly by society's rules. Vera keeps her feet on the ground while her brother remains distrustful, politicized, and voluble. It is as if Carolina divided her personality in two to live on in the next generation. Zé Carlos enthusiastically maintains that he is the rightful claimant to his mother's combatant spirit, yet we know that he has never demonstrated either her ambition or her discipline. His insistence about her legacy, however, is therapeutic for him, since he has fared so badly. His sister Vera has made a dignified, happy life for herself, in spite of her nightmares of favela life. Zé Carlos, in his sober moments, is charming, insightful, lucid, skillful at theatrics. He deserves our pity. Although his mother overcame far more hardship than her children had to and provided them with some small advantages, Zé Carlos's life nevertheless skidded away from him.

Interviews, even in-depth life history accounts, are of course fallible. Subjects have the opportunity to slant some past events, to suppress others, or to embellish. They may, if they wish, invent things out of whole cloth. Sometimes people remember what they want to remember, especially after years have passed. It may seem remarkable at first glance that both Vera and her brother recall many warm and positive things about their childhood, but this was the result of Carolina's heroic perseverance as a mother. Outsiders did not see this, but her children remember her good qualities as if she were still alive.

5

Carolina's Legacy

Although *Quarto de Despejo* touched a sensitive chord in Brazilian life in 1960, more than thirty years later critics still berated it. In November 1993, following the publication of the new Ática edition of *Quarto de Despejo*, the distinguished Brazilian literary scholar Wilson Martins dismissed the book as a "literary mystification" and a fake.[1] Martins attacked the book's "precious" language. He commented on Carolina's "casual lovers," as if her personal behavior canceled her right to be respected for her achievement. Moreover, he insinuated that Audálio Dantas had really written the book. Dantas's outraged reply was published only six weeks later in the same newspaper.[2]

Martins's scornful dismissal of Carolina's authenticity was as misinformed as it was insensitive. Comparing the surviving handwritten entries, not only of the diary pages that were the basis of *Quarto* but also the writings submitted posthumously to be published as *Diário de Bitita*, permits verification that Dantas and the other editors involved in publishing Carolina's writing *cut* material (mostly repetitive parts) but they did not substantially change her words.[3] What appeared in print was what Carolina Maria de Jesus thought and wrote during a twenty-year period of her life from the mid-1950s to her death. Her autobiographical writings, then, are influenced by memories likely embittered by the harsh reality of her life before she became famous and by her willfulness and difficult personality—attributes that caused her to squander her opportunities for advancement after the publication of her best-selling diary.

Carolina Maria de Jesus alienated others by refusing to moderate her opinions. She embarrassed people who publicly subscribed to the myth of Brazil's racial tolerance. Intellectuals displayed their own thinly-veiled prejudices by pointing out that Carolina herself was intolerant. "I walked with her in the street a few times," publisher Paulo Dantas said, "but I noted that she hated the common people. Perhaps this hatred inside her existed because it reminded her of things she wanted to forget."[4] Actually, Carolina criticized lazy blacks—namely the unemployed black migrants from the Northeast who lived in Canindé—but her writings are filled with expressions of pride in her blackness. She expressed sorrow for blacks who suffered hard lives because of the discrimination arrayed against them. Few took her side when she pointed out in her writing that blacks were still treated like slaves in Brazil, but during the 1988 Centenary of Abolition public debates, many black militants and academics made the same rhetorical point: slavery had never really been abolished.[5]

As literature, Carolina Maria de Jesus's published writing was not testimonial, but autobiographical. Testimonial literature speaks from the plural perspective ("I'd like to stress that it's not only *my* life, it's also the testimony of my people," Rigoberta Menchú's memoir says at the outset.)[6] More than anything else, the surprise of an unexpectedly detailed depiction of favela life by an uneducated black female—not the implications of the sufferings she described—was what in 1960 propelled unprecedented sales of the diary and gained celebrity status for its author. Since the wave of attention drummed up by television and the press focused on Carolina, and not on poverty and its causes, the book's success spawned only inconsequential debate about social realities. In turn, this lack of substance led the public to tire of Carolina quickly after her curiosity value diminished.

Few people understood the thickness of the protective shell that Carolina had been forced to construct around herself in response to decades of fierce adversity. Audálio Dantas did not remain her patron for long. Carolina, he insisted, would not accept the relationship he needed to impose on her as her agent. She never asked to be defended or cared for—she was too independent for that. Dantas explained that he could not deal with what he considered Carolina's petulance and irascibility. His opinion is consistent with that of other journalists and intellectuals who gave up on her. Perhaps it is also understandable that her diary continued to sell strongly outside of Brazil, where readers wanted to find in her words an expression of rage against poverty and suffering that Brazilians grew tired of because they considered her attitudes simplistic and self-serving. She was a product of a society that tolerated the most glaring maldistribution of income in the world; yet she did not lend her voice to calls for massive social change. She simply wanted to escape from poverty with her children and to become a famous writer.

Even though *Quarto* was a commercial success not only in São Paulo but in Rio de Janeiro and throughout Brazil, critics treated the book as an urban São Paulo phenomenon. In those parts of Brazil far removed from the specific conditions she wrote about, Carolina received even less critical notice. She quickly faded from the public spotlight in Brazil while her books continued to sell steadily in translation outside of the country. It still is difficult to understand how Carolina's star fell so swiftly. It seems extraordinary that no one in Brazil bothered to speak out against the trivialization to which she was subjected or to protest that the conditions Carolina had exposed merited greater national debate.

Critics blamed Carolina for failing to adjust to the middle-class life her success had made possible. Reporters who were sent to write about her consistently showed irritation that this black woman social critic was still a complainer. No one acknowledged that for a former slum dweller to have difficulty adjusting to a world which reviled people like her, was perfectly understandable. By emphasizing her brusqueness and eccentricities, the media deflected attention from what she was trying to say. They applied a double standard: after she became famous, reporters mocked her purchases of elegant clothing and her use of cosmetics. Yet when the novelist Patrícia Galvão (Pagú) dressed the same way two decades earlier, giving an even more garish impression, she became the darling of the cultural elite and of leftists. She was, after all, white, a member of the literary vanguard, the wife of modernist icon Oswald de Andrade, and a communist.[7]

Carolina Maria de Jesus's success in 1960 resulted in large part from fortuitous timing. Brazil had reached a crest of national optimism over economic development and populist reform, and many Brazilians saw Carolina as a symbol of hope. Brasília had just been completed. Brazil's beloved national soccer team had just won the 1960 World Cup. Many Brazilians believed that it was possible to bring about genuine social change. *Quarto de Despejo* and *Casa de Alvenaria* became powerful symbols of the belief that with help people could rise out of poverty and transform themselves. Carolina's personal honesty and her unwillingness to fall into despair contributed to the popular view of favela residents as "poor but honest."

One of her remarkable traits was her ability to relate to powerful people. Even though Brazil was a place where politicians did personal favors for ordinary people, employing this as a technique to win popularity, surely few indigent shantytown residents were on first-name terms with mayors and governors, as Carolina was well before she became famous. In 1954 Mayor Jânio Quadros arranged for her to have dentures fitted. Adhemar de Barros later sent her to the hospital after she was stabbed in the favela by a prostitute who attacked her son. There is something cruel about these interventions because the aid was so episodic. Once when she needed medicine she went to the Governor's Palace and was directed to the charity hospital, which refused her treatment. When she returned to the Palace to complain, she was thrown off the grounds by a soldier with a bayonet.[8] Most of the time, Carolina and her children lived on the edge of starvation and the politicians did nothing to help her then. When her children were sick she had to treat them with roots and other home remedies because she had no money for medicine, even in Parelheiros. She complained about this paradox in *Quarto de Despejo*. The city health department, she wrote, held clinics to test poor residents for parasitic disease, and told them how to cure it. But there was no money to buy the medicine, so the people remained infested.[9]

Another of Carolina's unappreciated traits was her practical view of national affairs. She diligently read newspapers, even when she had to pluck them out of the gutter. Like many poor Brazilians, she admired Getúlio Vargas, although much of Vargas's populism was manipulative and he actually did little to merit the adulation of the destitute. A select few received jobs and social benefits, and the vast majority received benign neglect. Carolina understood how the system worked, and bluntly said so—although she always loved Brazil, and considered herself a good citizen. In the rare instances that politicians did address poverty, she noted in her diaries, their efforts were insincere and disappeared after election time.[10]

Carolina's description in her autobiographical writings of her reaction to the events of 1930 was aided by hindsight, since she wrote when she was an adult, but it remains the most detailed account of Vargas's impact among the rural poor in the entire literature of Brazilian political history:[11]

One day I awoke confused to see the streets filled with soldiers. It was a revolution. . . . The people only talked about Getúlio Vargas and [vice-presidential candidate] João Pessoa. . . . With Getúlio Vargas we will have more work. . . . The soldiers spread through the streets with green, yellow, and white banners with Getúlio's face in the center. Those who saw the portrait liked him and said: "Now Brazil will be watched over by a man!" This will move the country forward. . . . Our country is very backward."

She followed these lines with a poem:

Long live our Revolution
Brazil will ascend like a balloon
With Getúlio, Brazil moves ahead
With Getúlio, Brazil won't fall.
Let's have more bread on the table
Getúlio is a friend of the poor.

She continued:

People said that the Revolution wanted residents of the countryside to go to the cities, to find work in the factories. Factory work didn't require skills: that's it. Digging tools were abandoned and ploughs stopped being used. Brazil would stop being an agricultural nation and transform itself into an industrialized country. The people said that Getúlio Vargas would give loans to entrepreneurs who wanted to start industries. It was the first time in the history of Brazil that a president gave incentives to the people to recover their self-respect. The poor people said: Getúlio will be our beacon. . . . After the conflict ended, they turned in their Bonus coupons and received in exchange 100 mil-réis, that in those days was worth a fortune . . . when someone had this in their pocket, he had the impression he was almost a banker. They were men tranquil for not having economic problems."[12]

Carolina credited Brazil's new president with giving rural youths the opportunity to migrate to São Paulo by drafting them into the service and sending them away from the hardscrabble interior. These young men got jobs in São Paulo, she said, a place that for her was "heaven's waiting room." She credited Vargas for reanimating people who were lukewarm, apathetic, idealistic dreamers. Now they were motivated because they believed that "this government would not deceive them." Businessmen, she declared, said that they were going to São Paulo to get a loan from Getúlio and open a plant with fifty workers because Getúlio said that if workers have jobs they won't have time to go astray. "Not only does he give us loans, she wrote, "but his goal is to make workers the beneficiaries. Industry in São Paulo brings immediate profits."

Quarto de Despejo likely would not have been published at all if Carolina's diaries had been discovered before 1958 or after 1961. Juscelino Kubitschek's successor in the presidency in 1960 was the mercurial Jânio Quadros. He resigned abruptly in 1961 and fled the country when his government became paralyzed in the midst of rising tensions. His successor was João Goulart, who further polarized politics and heightened ideological rhetoric. In this climate, Carolina's diary would have been dismissed as being too naive. The military dictatorship that seized power by overthrowing Goulart in 1964 was little interested in social reforms. It initiated an era of Chicago-School economic development that greatly increased the disparity between rich and poor and left many Brazilians feeling helpless and angry.[13] When the black performer Josephine Baker visited Brazil in 1971 after an absence of twenty years, she was staggered by the poverty she saw, especially by black beggar women with infants in their arms. Once when she was sitting in an elegant outdoor Copacabana cafe, a poor woman with a child approached her table. Josephine Baker took the child in her arms and collected money from her hosts for the woman. "Don't do it, they told her: these beggars rent children for the day to win sympathy."[14]

What Baker was seeing was a Brazilian society that had become more divided than ever between an affluent world of whites and an almost universally marginalized world of blacks and persons of mixed racial ancestry. Women fared much less well than men in this world. Until 1988, Brazilian civil laws clearly discriminated against women. Before a battered wife could press charges against her husband, he had to give his written permission.[15] Carolina was a poor black woman possessing an iron will and a strong sense of what she wanted. She was aware of the legacies of racism, gender prejudice, and political neglect of the marginalized and the oppressed, but she dealt with these burdens only as they directly affected her.

Of the three conceptual and empirical categories that organize experience and perception in Brazil—gender, class, and race[16]—Carolina was most often discussed by Brazilians in terms of her indigence. Remarkably few references to her in the press at the time she became a celebrity referred to her blackness, although it was patently obvious that her race had set her apart. Fewer still commented on the fact that she was a woman. Carolina always had to struggle harder because she was a female. Observers expressed irritation when she—in their words— "dragged" her children along with her, as if she had somewhere safe to leave them. "Proper" Brazilians did not know what to make of an assertive black woman who lacked social graces. Moreover, there is little doubt that critics and even some early supporters were so quick to dismiss her because she was seen as an uppity woman, and an uppity black woman at that. For one thing, males from similar backgrounds would not have been ostracized because of their sexual activities. Yet many of her male critics belittled her sexual promiscuity, especially her relationships with white men.

One of the reasons that Brazilian society disparaged Carolina's preference for white men was that it violated an unwritten code that judged it entirely unacceptable for a black woman to initiate and control sexual choice. White men could choose dark-skinned sexual partners, especially if the women were unusually attractive. But these were liaisons, not marriages. Men could proposition dark-complexioned women (as many did Carolina while she was considered physically attractive) but not vice versa. Carolina's desire to have lovers but not submit to a husband (in a culture rampant with marital violence against poor women) also annoyed her critics. Yet in other ways, Carolina's environment shaped her. She was submissive when she dealt with men. Both Dantases commented on this, and so did her children.

The lives of females are often seen as more trivial and less important that the lives of males.[17] Women internalize this view, diminishing their self-esteem as a result of social pressure. This was certainly not the case with Carolina Maria de Jesus. She commented succinctly and matter-of-factly on the disadvantages being a woman added to the other obstacles in her path as an indigent, unskilled black migrant. That she was a mother who self-confidently brought up her children amidst squalor, insisting that her children be honest, moral, and attend school, was entirely lost on those who judged her. That Carolina was denied consideration of her basic rights as a citizen was never considered worthy of comment, even by reform-minded journalists, after the publication of her diary. The plight of impoverished women was not considered important enough to create outrage over the failure to enforce laws devoted to those who most needed relief and protection.

As a poor black Brazilian woman, Carolina faced deplorable prejudice. Prior to her discovery by Audálio Dantas, one of the first editors to whom she submitted her writing told her that she should write on toilet paper.[18] Given Carolina's unprecedented achievement, it is difficult to understand why so few women rose to her defense when attacks began after the first, flushed days of her fame. Female Brazilian journalists generally treated her as harshly, or more harshly, than did their male counterparts. Few members of Brazil's women's movement in the 1970s and 1980s had ever heard of her. Typically, however, they cried out against Brazilian cultural conventions that justified the forced obedience of wives to husbands based on the common belief that women were born to suffer, that *mulher não é gente* ("women are not people"). *Women in Brazil*, a passionate, angry indictment of sexism published in 1993, devoted major emphasis to racism and the need for Brazilian women to find new role models. The book entirely ignores Carolina, although it quotes the later diary of another black *favela* woman, Anna Lúcia Florisbela dos Santos. This work is startlingly similar in its summary of conditions to Carolina's diary written a generation earlier.[19]

Nothing is known about Carolina's younger brother—we lose track of him in Minas Gerais—but we can speculate that as an uneducated, spurned, poor rural black he likely lived a life of destitution. Still, if Carolina had been a man and therefore had not been considered unemployable in São Paulo after her first pregnancy, she might not have ended up in a favela. The disdain directed at Carolina after her publishing success was a predictable response to an unconstrained, outspoken black female. Soccer star Romário, the luminary of Brazil's 1994 World Cup champions, displayed more petulant and rude behavior than Carolina ever did—in one widely-quoted interview, for example, he called Pelé (Brazil's greatest soccer hero) "mentally retarded"—but journalists shrugged off this rudeness as an attribute of Romário's *machismo*. Had Carolina spoken out half as aggressively as Romário, she would have been crucified by the press, not merely deprecated.

Throughout her life, Carolina was weighed down by the scorn heaped upon her by society. Even though she shielded herself and her children from the squalid aspects of slum life, these conditions took their toll. By the time she was liberated from the favela by a stroke of fate, it was too late. She was exhausted, too beaten down to learn middle-class manners, to censor her thoughts, to remove the layers of suffering from her psyche, or to prescribe solutions for society's ills.

Hostility to her blackness, as well, plagued Carolina ceaselessly. Educated Brazilians accepted the myth of Brazilian racial democracy, despite the obvious evidence of racism surrounding them, especially discrimination against people of very dark skin.[20] Carolina's autobiographical writings describe racist incidents constantly, almost matter-of-factly, long before other Brazilians acknowledged racial prejudice. Foreigners less influenced by the Brazilian racial mythology often recognized race prejudice when they visited Brazil. The Hollywood film director Orson Welles, invited in 1941 to participate in a birthday celebration broadcast for dictator Getúlio Vargas, was told that he could not bring a black friend with him into the studio. Welles' attempts to film *It's All True,* an anthology film with segments about Brazilian Carnival and the plight of northeastern raft fishermen, was criticized in a secret letter from Welles's Brazilian production manager to the police complaining about Welles's "insistence on emphasizing the unsavory Negro element and mixture of the races."[21]

The attacks on Carolina were never seen by Brazilians as examples of anti-black prejudice or discrimination against poor women. At a meeting in December 1992 in São Paulo of students who had read *Quarto de Despejo* for the first time, respondents identified her a "social victim," "a marginal," a "favela dweller," not as a black when asked to describe the author.[22] Not a single participant recalled the passages in her book in which she expressed her pride in being black or her statement that if she were born again she still would want to be black. Students in the United States, on the other hand, invariably pick up on these issues.

From the days of her childhood to her final years in self-exile, Carolina's response was to distance herself from others, in order to maintain control over her life. This trait, in fact, was in many ways the key to her ability to keep her sanity. Her writing was her life; her work kept her spirit alive.[23] This helps explain why she was so much of an outcast. She was the one who persisted in reading when others played. She was the one who refused to drink alcohol or to gossip or give in to hopelessness. She decided when to pack up and move on—from Sacramento when she sought medical treatment, and later when she joined the migratory stream of thousands of other rural women who shared her plight.

Carolina's insistence on controlling her life is demonstrated by her independence with employers and also by her refusal to wed, even if marriage might have brought her greater economic security. She knew that a husband would dominate her because this was the way of Brazilian society. She sought out men whose liaisons with her would be temporary, or so socially unacceptable that they could never expect to dominate her. To maintain control of her life, she limited her friendships, accepting only those people, like Maria Puerta and Mariazinha, who respected her completely and maintained a discreet distance. More than any other example of Carolina's insistence on preserving her independence was the way she refused to be dominated by Audálio Dantas, her discoverer and would-be mentor whom she called her Svengali. Dantas was the most dangerous of all of the people who entered her life because he offered the most seductive and generous rewards if she relinquished her control over her destiny. Deep inside, given her stubborn belief that she had to maintain control at all costs, Carolina believed that she had to cut off any relationships that threatened to affect her and her children. This stubbornness served as a coping skill common to the most destitute, and in Carolina's case the trait in many ways served her well.

The precise disposition of Carolina's income from the initial publication of her diary remains unclear. It was true, as her detractors were quick to point out, that she did not know how to manage her money. She spent a good deal on new clothing. Photographs of her during her period of fame, however, do not support the allegation that she dressed outlandishly. It was just that Brazilians were unaccustomed to the notion of a woman from a favela shopping on Rua Augusta, São Paulo's Fifth Avenue. It was also likely true that she was a soft touch for hardship stories, and a bad businesswoman. More than anything else, though, she did achieve her main goal in life—to escape from the favela and to give her children opportunities she never had, without hunger at the door.

Even if Carolina's words awakened the consciousness of readers around the world about the plight of Brazil's slum dwellers, a generation later things had only worsened. Violent crime, gangs, and drug infestation of favelas—as well as the continually widening gap between rich and poor in Brazil—made it ever more difficult for families at the bottom of society to improve their lives. "We suffer the same in whichever favela we live," observed Beti, a resident of Rio's Rocinha shantytown city in 1984, echoing the sentiments of *Quarto de Despejo*; "when we have water, there is no soap. When we have soap, there is no water."[24]

In the United States, Carolina's diary was but one of what critics have described, in the 1990s, as a growing "good and valuable stream of . . . books recapturing the life experiences" of blacks.[25] No such stream has yet appeared in Brazil. There, Carolina Maria de Jesus became a heroine for a small group of marginalized black intellectuals, and lives vaguely in the memory of scattered groups of poor black women. She did not become "the hope for her community." Her favela experiences, so painstakingly recorded, have never been considered relevant; her painful, extraordinarily detailed autobiographical writings about her childhood have been entirely ignored. Carolina died a broken woman, forgotten in Brazil, her miseries only fractionally relieved, her remarkable life overlooked. She had lived independently with a self-sufficiency that was taken as a rebuke, but she had never lost her way. She stubbornly refused to accept what was considered to be the role of the poor, and especially poor women, to suffer in silence.[26] Many rejected her because once she became prominent, she seemed to them "common" and "ordinary" in the way she behaved. For a society like Brazil's, where being "ordinary" is not admired, few were able to recognize that she was, in fact, an extraordinary human being.

Final Thoughts

We explained in the introductory chapter that one of the intriguing aspects of this research project for the co-authors was the fact that at the outset each held divergent views about the significance of Carolina's life and death and her writing. Some of the differences stemmed from the separate traditions of race relations in Brazil and in the United States. The latter tradition is rooted in the early nineteenth-century triumph of liberalism in the United States and the country's evolving democratic tradition. In Brazil, Sebe observed, race was traditionally seen in terms of individuals, not as an issue for government or institutional intervention. This fact explains Carolina's first diary's inability to spur extensive action to combat the causes of favela misery. Carolina's Brazilianness, moreover,

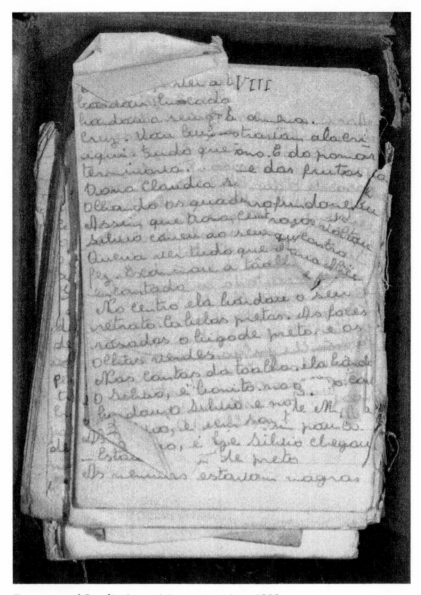

Fragments of Carolina's surviving manuscripts, 1993.
Photo by Robert M. Levine.

is incidental to her popularity outside of Brazil. American culture celebrates struggle—even failed struggle—against fate, while Brazilian culture judges this behavior as egotism or foolishness.

In the course of writing this book, the ways each of us as co-authors have looked at Carolina and her significance have converged. We are highly sympathetic to her and to her plight and admire her resourcefulness. Carolina's complex personality reflected the battering she took throughout her life but her acute powers of observation taught her how the system worked and how to survive on her own terms. Her personality, of course, was buffeted by extremes. Sometimes she was exuberant, even romantic. At other times, her understanding of the hopelessness of her misery triggered depression. She admired the rich but remained loyal to members of her pariah caste—as long as they conformed to her high moral standards.

Foreign readers captivated by her story usually are not aware of the debate among Brazilian critics over the extent to which her diary was a "product" of Audálio Dantas—although we know that he edited her writing heavily but did not put words into her mouth. Foreigners should not use Carolina's writings to form a picture in their minds of Brazilian poverty today because poverty in Brazil is vastly different from the 1950s when Carolina started her diary entries. But Brazilian intellectuals are dead wrong when they disparage her importance, lumping her into their prejudiced view of favelados as *malandros* (trouble-makers). They are ignorant of the fact that Carolina's writing is stilted not because someone doctored it but because that was the style of expression, rooted in archaic Portuguese, where she grew up in rural Minas Gerais.

Our book presents two main explanations for Carolina's life trajectory. One is that Carolina was the victim of racism and sexism; the other is that her difficult personality and willfulness led her to squander her opportunities for advancement. We challenge the notion that her life was, especially after her descent from celebrity, a failure. Carolina did achieve the self-pride and personal autonomy she had consistently sought since her childhood. Her fierce independence was the natural result of an upbringing in which her father abandoned her and her cringing mother admonished her to be servile and to suppress her ambitions amidst the casual brutality of a rural society that flourished in ignorance.

In spite of these traumas, and the ultimate loss of her employability in São Paulo as a maid in homes of the rich because of her "crime" of bearing children, she persevered in the face of daunting obstacles. Intelligent but little-educated, she fought to keep herself informed so that she could understand the world beyond the favela. In this quest for autonomy and self-esteem, other people, including benefactors and friends, were potential threats because they did not understand her all-consuming goal of control over her life on her own terms. Although clearly swept away by her fame and good fortune after her diary was published, she remained wary and distrustful of those who sought to guide her. That is, she consciously or unconsciously behaved in ways that subverted her material success on the way to achieving greater independence for herself and her children. Her life was not a waste. She took uncommon pleasure in what she had done, in her writing, in her children, and especially in her decision to cut herself off from the world that had closed in on her before she departed for Parelheiros to spend her final years in solace.[27]

Notes

Notes to Preface

1. For useful discussions of the problems created by interviewing persons of lower social and economic standing, especially when the interviewers but not their subjects are educated, see Sherna Berger Gluck and Daphne Patai, *Women's Words: The Feminist Practice of Oral History* (New York: Routledge, 1991), especially the essays by Kathryn Anderson and Dana C. Jack, "Learning to Listen," 11–26, and Karen Olson and Linda Shopes, "Crossing Boundaries, Building Bridges: Doing Oral History among Working-Class Women and Men," 189–204; Inderpal Grewal and Caren Kaplan, eds., *Scattered Hegemonies: Postmodernity and Transnational Feminist Practices* (Minneapolis: University of Minnesota Press, 1994); and Frances O'Gorman e Mulheres da Rocinha e da Santa Maria, *Morro, Mulher* (São Paulo: Edições Paulinas, 1984).
2. *Latin American Research Review*, 29:1 (1994): 55–84; *Cinderela Negra: A Saga de Carolina Maria de Jesus* (Rio de Janeiro: Editora UFRJ, 1994).

Notes to Chapter 1

1. Linda Wagner-Martin, *Telling Women's Lives; the New Biography* (New Brunswick, NJ: Rutgers University Press, 1994), 29.
2. *Child of the Dark: The Diary of Carolina Maria de Jesus*, (New York: Mentor Books, 1962), 37.
3. Barbara Harlow and Claudia Salazar observe that most Third World women's autobiographies tend to allocate the private and domestic experiences of the narrator to the historical and public context of their personal struggles—exemplified by Menchú's *I . . . Rigoberta Menchú: An Indian Woman in Guatemala*, trans. Ann Wright (London: Verso, 1984)—but Carolina Maria de Jesus did not do this. See Barbara Harlow, *Resistance Literature* (New York: Methuen, 1987); Claudia Salazar, "A Third World Woman's Text: Between the Politics of Criticism and Cultural Politics," in Gluck and Patai,

eds., *Women's Words*, 93–106. Menchú won the Nobel Prize for her harrowing tales of brutality against Native Guatemalans and for her international campaign to curb such abuses.

Notes to Chapter 2

1. Diretoria Geral de Estatística, *Recenseamentos*, 226–27, 647 (1920); 79 (1950). The 1920 census enumerated 33,866 people, 26,855 of them unable to read and write.
2. On other occasions, she was described as having been born as early as 1913 and as late as 1921. See Célia Pisa, introduction to the French translation Le Dépotoir (Paris: Éditions A.-M. Métaillié, 1982), 7; Robert Collin, "Elle a écrit un best-seller," *Le Monde*, archived at *O Globo* (Rio de Janeiro).
3. The trolleys ran until the 1930s, when the municipality liquidated them. See Antonio Pereira da Silva, "Os Bondes Caipiras de Sacramento," *D. O. Leitura* (January 12, 1994), 3–4. Carolina wrote about this in one of her unpublished short stories.
4. Three years after Carolina's death, more than half of Brazil's non-white population remained illiterate or semi-literate. See Sueli Carneiro, Thereza Santos, and Albertina Gordo de Oliveira Costa, *Mulher Negra: Política Governamental e a Mulher* (São Paulo: Nobel, 1985), 6.
5. The image of nature performing for her because she was too poor to pay for entertainment occurred frequently in Carolina's published diary in 1960. Her memoirs, of course, were written a decade after the diary was published.
6. Carolina Maria de Jesus, "Fatal Intervention," an autobiographical short story, manuscript courtesy of her daughter, Vera Eunice de Jesus Lima. All further quotations from Carolina's autobiographical writings, some of which were incorporated into her book *Diário de Bitita*, come from these manuscripts, typed from the originals by Vera after her mother's death.
7. Paraphrased from Vera Jesus de Lima's typed copies of her mother's handwritten memoirs. Some of this material was later published in *Diário de Bitita* although it was virtually ignored when the book appeared.
8. On the migration of women from Brazil's rural interior to the city, see Lorene Y. L. Yap, "The Attraction of Cities: A Review of the Migration Literature," *Journal of Development Economics*, 4 (1977): 239–264.
9. Regina Penteado, "Carolina, vítima ou louca?" *Folha de São Paulo*, December 1, 1976, 31.
10. See Nabil G. Bonduki, "The Housing Crisis in the Postwar Years," in Lúcio Kowarick, ed., *Social Struggles and the City: The Case of São Paulo* (New York: Monthly Review Press, 1994), 94–120.
11. *O Globo* (Rio de Janeiro), October 24, 1972; David St. Clair, translator's preface to *Child of the Dark: The Diary of Carolina Maria de Jesus* (New York: Mentor Books, 1962), 8–9. Further references to Carolina's diary will be cited from *Child of the Dark*, not *Quarto de Despejo*, to aid English-speaking readers.
12. See Lúcio Kowarick and Nabil G. Bonduki, "Urban Space and Political Space: From Populism to Redemocratization," in Lúcio Kowarick, ed., *Social Struggles and the City*, 121–47, especially note 7, p. 147.
13. Paulo Dantas, in his interview (February 2, 1993), called the man "Davis."

14. St. Clair, translator's preface to *Child of the Dark*, 10. St. Clair says 1943; he likely meant 1953.
15. *Child of the Dark*, 142.
16. For a scholarly study of migrants from the interior to São Paulo favelas, see Richard A. Gorell, "Families in Shantytowns in São Paulo, Brazil, 1945–1984: the Rural-Urban Connection" (Ph.D. diss., University of Kansas, 1990).
17. Melvin S. Arrington, Jr., "From the Garbage Dump to the Brick House," *Southeastern Latin Americanist*, 36:4 (Spring 1993): 1–12, especially 2.
18. *Folha da Manhã* (São Paulo), February 24, 1941.
19. *Child of the Dark*, 42.
20. See Daphne Patai, introduction to *Brazilian Women Speak* (New Brunswick: Rutgers University Press, 1988), 1–35.
21. *Child of the Dark*, 37.
22. Interview, Marta Teresinha Godinho, São Paulo, January 18, 1993.
23. I am grateful to Cristina Mehrtens for this observation.
24. *Child of the Dark*, 44.
25. *Child of the Dark*, 114.
26. *Child of the Dark*, 36, 47.
27. Audálio Dantas, interview with Janes Jorge, São Paulo, October 5, 1992.
28. St. Clair, translator's preface to *Child of the Dark*, 12.
29. St. Clair, translator's preface to *Child of the Dark*, 12. Juliano Spyer observes that Carolina's diary entries for the years 1955–58 may have been sparse when Dantas read them, and that he may have worked with her to add material retrospectively.
30. Quoted in Carlos Rangel, "Após a Glória, Solidão e Felicidade," *Folha de São Paulo*. June 29, 1975, Arq. *Folha de São Paulo*.
31. See Robert M. Levine, *Vale of Tears: The Canudos Massacre in Northeastern Brazil, 1893–1897* (Berkeley and London: University of California Press, 1992).
32. Paulo Dantas interview, São Paulo, February 2, 1993.
33. The publisher did put some effort into the design, however, employing Ciro del Nero, a well-known illustrator, to design the cover and provide drawings.
34. Carolina Maria de Jesus, *Casa de Alvenaria*, 11.
35. We are grateful to Thomas Holloway for these insights. He notes that Audálio Dantas uses the metaphor of the Garbage Room in his preface when he refers to people "in their parlors turning up their noses at the smell coming from the trash room."
36. Audálio Dantas, "Nossa Irmã Carolina," preface to *Quarto de Despejo* (Rio de Janeiro: Francisco Alves, 1960), 11. He omitted mention of her two sons.
37. *Child of the Dark*, 78, 84.
38. *Child of the Dark*, 120.
39. *Child of the Dark*, 25.
40. *Child of the Dark*, 31.
41. *Child of the Dark*, 35.
42. *Child of the Dark*, 35.
43. *Child of the Dark*, 229.
44. *Child of the Dark*, 105.

45. Copies were sold exclusively at Livraria Francisco Alves for a week; then they were released to other booksellers; St. Clair, translator's preface to *Child of the Dark*, 12.
46. *O Estado de São Paulo*, February 14, 1977, archived at *O Globo*.
47. The most successful of these books—dictated by their authors to professional writers—were Elizabeth Burgos-Debray's *Me Llamo Rigoberta Menchú* (Barcelona, 1983; São Paulo, 1984), and Brazilian-born Moema Viezzer's 1982 book, *Se Me Deixam Falar . . . Depoimento de uma Mineira Boliviana*, 14th ed. (São Paulo: Ed. Global, 1990), the story of the life of a miner's wife. Neither one, interestingly, was about a Brazilian woman. For a theoretical discussion of the interventionist aspect of editors of testimonies by unlettered or lower class subjects, see Claudia Salazar, "A Third World Woman's Text: Between the Politics and Criticism and Cultural Politics," in Gluck and Patai, eds., *Women's Words*, 93–106, esp. 98–99.
48. Notarized Contract, Liv. Francisco Alves, 1960 (date is unclear from xerox copy of contract). Courtesy Claudio Lacerda and Nélida Piñón.
49. St. Clair, translator's preface to *Child of the Dark*, 14; *Time*, 76:13 (September 26, 1960), 43.
50. "Carolina mudou de casa sem promover despejo," *Folha da Manhã* (São Paulo), December 25, 1960, clipping found in a copy of an autographed copy of *Casa de Despejo* purchased for the equivalent of 75 cents by José Carlos Sebe Bom Meihy on December 22, 1992.
51. Maria de Lourdes Teixeira, "Diario da Fome," *Manchete*, c. 1960, p. 10. archived at *O Globo*.
52. See, for example. "Da favela para a fama," *O Globo*, February 14, 1977, archived at *O Globo*.
53. Ignacio de Loyola, "Estou cansada de tudo," *Ultima Hora* (Rio de Janeiro), March 20, 1961, 8.
54. *Tribuna de Imprensa* (Rio de Janeiro), March 10, 1961. archived at *O Globo*.
55. *Tribuna de Imprensa* (Rio de Janeiro), March 10, 1961. archived *O Globo*.
56. *Casa de Alvenaria*, p. 118.
57. Quoted by Neide Ricosti, "Carolina de Jesus," *Manchete*, April 21, 1973, n.a., archived at *O Globo*.
58. *O Globo*, archived at *O Globo*; Carlos Rangel, "Após a Glória, Solidão e Felicidade," *Folha de São Paulo*, June 29, 1975, archived at *Folha de São Paulo*.
59. Carlos Vogt, "Trabalho, pobreza e trabalho intelectual (O *Quarto de Despejo*, de Carolina Maria de Jesus)," in Robert Schwartz, *Os pobres na literatura brasileira* (São Paulo: Brasiliense, 1983), 204–213, 204.
60. Prefeitura do Município de São Paulo, *Desfavelamento do Canindé* (São Paulo: Divisão de Serviço Social, São Paulo, July 1962), 3–4.
61. Carolina Maria de Jesus, *Casa de Alvenaria*, 90.
62. Quoted in St. Clair, translator's preface to *Child of the Dark*, 15.
63. Audálio Dantas interview, October 5, 1992.
64. Carolina Maria de Jesus, *Casa de Alvenaria*, 109.
65. Carolina Maria de Jesus, *Casa de Alvenaria*, 183. Suplicy in later years became the first senator elected by the Workers' Party, the PT. In 1992, known for his ethical behavior, he lost a race for mayor of São Paulo to Paulo Maluf.

66. Audálio Dantas interview, October 5, 1992.
67. The addendum was never published in Brazil.
68. Carolina Maria de Jesus, *Casa de Ladrillos* (Buenos Aires: Editorial Abraxas, 1963), 133.
69. Audálio Dantas, interview, October 5, 1992.
70. Paulo Dantas, interview, February 2, 1993.

Notes to Chapter 3

1. See John D. French, "Workers and the Rise of Adhemarista Populism in São Paulo, Brazil, 1945–47," *Hispanic American Historical Review*, 68:1 (February 1988): 1–43.
2. Statements published in frontpiece to Carolina Maria de Jesus, *Casa de Alvenaria*. (Rio de Janeiro: Livraria Francisco Alves, 1961).
3. Elias Raide, cited in Regina Penteado, "Carolina, vítima ou louca?" *Folha de São Paulo*, December 1, 1976, 31.
4. José Franco, "Dona Zulmira: Guardiã dos pobres," *O Cruzeiro* (Rio de Janeiro), December 9, 1961, 57–58. As recently as October 1993, the popular national television variety show "Fantástico" interviewed a black cleaning woman employed at São Paulo's main railroad station. She once had been famous in Brazil and in Europe as a ballerina dancer.
5. José Franco, "Dona Zulmira: Guardiã dos pobres," 58.
6. See George Reid Andrews, *Black and White in São Paulo*, (Madison: University of Wisconsin Press, 1991). Her conservatism and her emphasis on food, not race, may have alienated her from intellectuals. See also *Child of the Dark*, 21, 30, 52–52, 58, 122.
7. Oscar Lewis, *Children of Sánchez* (New York: Vintage, 1963) and *Five Families: Case Studies in the Culture of Poverty* (New York: New American Library, 1965).
8. *Tagebuch der Armut: Aufzeichnungen einer brasilianischen Negerin* (1962) was originally translated by Johannes Gerold. Information about the German editions courtesy of Dr. Jens Hentschke. See faxed letter from Jörg Stöckli, Liepman AG, to Jens Hentschke, Zurich; faxed letter from Lark-Klaus Rabe, Lamuv, to Jens Hentschke, Göttingen, February 11, 1993; faxed letter from Lilo Sauer, Buchverlage Ullstein Langen Müller/ Nymphenburger Verglagsanstalt, to Jens Hentschke, Munich, April 13, 1993. All held as personal correspondence by Robert M. Levine.
9. Wegner sent royalties to Liepman Zurich, which divided it according to the various contracts: Liepman and Catalina W. de Wulff were to have received 5% each, with the remaining 90% to go to de Wulff again (80%) and Wegner (20%), De Wulff had negotiated with Romiglio de Giacompol in São Paulo, a friend of Audálio Dantas's and the broker for all of these book subcontracts. See faxed letters, Jens Hentschke to Robert M. Levine, Rostock, March 26, 1993 and Oxford, October 22, 1993. Also, E-mail, Juliano Spyer to Robert M. Levine, April 8, 1993 (reporting Vera's comments). According to Jörg Stöckli (Liepman AG), Wegner published the diary in the first half of 1962, selling at least 7,427 copies (based on incomplete records). On the basis of the sub-agreements with Wegner, Fischer was allowed to publish 22,000 books and Reclam Junior 20,000 for its first edition in 1965. Con-

cerning Reclam's second edition, the dates are contradictory: while the publishing house itself speaks of 15,000 books, Liepman is not sure about the contracts. Either 10,000 or 15,000 books were sold. For Deutsche Buchgemeinschaft no dates are available.

10. Carlos Vogt, "Trabalho, pobreza e trabalho intelectual (O *Quarto de Despejo*, de Carolina Maria de Jesus)," in Robert Schwartz, org., *Os pobres na literatura brasileira* (São Paulo: Brasiliense, 1983), 204–213, 206.

11. Alcidez Fernández, interview, São Paulo, January 7, 1993.

12. *Niger*, 1: 3 (September 1960), reprinted in José Correia Leite & Cuti (Luiz Silva), ...*E Disse o Velho Militante José Correia Leite* (São Paulo: Prefeitura do Município de São Paulo/ Secretaria Municipal de Cultura, 1992), 180. I am indebted to Anani Dzidzienyo of Brown University for calling this book to my attention. For a broad view of the history of race relations in São Paulo, see Andrews, *Blacks and Whites in São Paulo.*

13. José Correia Leite & Cuti, ...*E Disse*, 182–83.

14. Audálio Dantas, preface to *Casa de Alvenaria: História de uma Ascensão Social* (São Paulo: Livraria Francisco Alves, 1961), 5.

15. *Casa de Alvenaria*, 83. See M. S. Arrington, Jr., "From the Garbage Dump," 7.

16. Paulo Dantas interview, Feb. 2, 1993.

17. *Casa de Alvenaria*, 135.

18. Carolina Maria de Jesus, *Casa de Alvenaria*, 2. 96.

19. Audálio Dantas interview, October 5, 1992.

20. Rangel, "Após a glória, solidão e felicidade."

21. *Herald Tribune* and *Horizon* quotes are taken from back jacket of Mentor edition of *Child of the Dark.*

22. Penteado, "Carolina, vítima ou louca?"

23. Alberto Moravia, preface to Carolina de Jesus, *Quarto de Despejo* [title of the Italian edition] (Milan: Valentino Bompiani, 1962), 6–7.

24. Mario Trejo, Prologue to *La Favela: Casa de Desahogo* (Havana: Casa de las Americas, 1989), vii.

25. Nobuo Hamaguchi, *Karorina no Nikki* [Carolina's Diary], 3rd ed. (Tokyo: Kawade-Shobou-Sinsha), 1962. Information courtesy of Professor Shigeru Suzuki.

26. *Provérbios* (São Paulo: Gráfica Editora Luzes, Ltda., 1965). See Melvin S. Arrington, Jr., "Gnomic Literature from the *Favela*: The *Provérbios* of Carolina Maria de Jesus," *Romance Notes*, 34:1 (1993), 79–85.

27. *O Globo* (Rio de Janeiro), December 11, 1969, archived at *O Globo.*

28. Carolina Maria de Jesus, *Diário de Bitita* (Rio de Janeiro: Nova Fronteira, 1986).

29. *Diário de Bitita*, 64.

30. The Brazilian edition of *Diário de Bitita* acknowledges the fact that the Paris publisher held the copyright.

31. *Diário de Bitita*, 7.

32. *Diário de Bitita*, 27.

33. *Diário de Bitita*, 38.

34. *Diário de Bitita*, 46.

35. *Diário de Bitita*, 52.

36. *Diário de Bitita*, 59.

37. *O Globo* (Rio de Janeiro), December 11, 1969, archived at *O Globo*. According to the newspaper article, she did not reply "to avoid further scandal."

38. *O Globo* (Rio de Janeiro), December 11, 1969, archived at *O Globo*. The lot was 8,000 square meters in size.

39. *O Globo* (Rio de Janeiro). December 11, 1969, archived at *O Globo*; Neide Ricosti, "Carolina de Jesus," *Manchete*, April 21, 1973, n.p., archived at *O Globo*; *Jornal do Brasil*, February 14, 1977, archived at *O Globo*. The term *caboclo* generally meant a person with mixed Indian and Caucasian blood but in the sense of the newspaper article it clearly meant a black. It was used in the sense of Monteiro Lobato's use of the term, to connote laziness and lack of industry.

40. *Folha de São Paulo*, February 9, 1970, archived at *Folha de São Paulo*.

41. Neide Ricosti, "Carolina de Jesus," *Manchete*, April 21, 1976, n.p., archived at *O Globo*.

42. Carolina claimed that she had purchased copies of the Brazilian edition from time to time in used bookstores, but that people had stolen them from her when they visited her house; Rangel, "Após a glória, solidão e felicidade."

43. *Loc. cit.*

44. *Loc. cit.*

45. Penteado, "Carolina, vítima ou louca?" 31.

46. José Carlos de Jesus, letter to *Folha de São Paulo Ilustrada*, February 20, 1977, archived at *Folha de São Paulo*.

47. *O Estado de São Paulo*, February 14, 1977, archived at *O Globo*. A third effort was made to make a movie about Carolina's life in the mid-1980s, when an American screenwriter wrote a full-length screenplay about Carolina's life. Again, nothing came of it. See Karen Brown, screenplay of "Passion Flower: The Story of Carolina Maria de Jesus," Los Angeles, 1991, lent to authors by Vera Eunice de Jesus Lima. The screenplay, anticipating a Hollywood treatment, glamorized Carolina ridiculously, making her into a sensual young woman and emphasizing the lyrical character of her story.

48. Exchange rate courtesy of Cristina Mehrtens. Rio's *Ultima Hora* said that the book, having gone through eight editions, had made Cr$ 2,050,000 in royalties for Carolina (March 20, 1961), 8.

49. She singled out for blame a Mr. [Ernest] Miller, who arranged for author's rights from various countries, and "Romiglio Jean Compoff" (probably an inaccurate version of Romiglio Giacompol's name), who had arranged for the rights in Germany and Italy. Cited in Penteado, "Carolina, vítima ou louca?," 31. Miller, she told another reporter, "took a good deal of advantage." The Argentine agent, "Juan Compol," she said, "vanished". Again she was likely referring to Dantas's friend Romiglio Giacompol. See *Jornal do Brasil*, December 11, 1976, archived at *O Globo*. Audálio Dantas, who according to Regina Penteado asked Regina not to publish the names, said that Miller, who spoke several languages, had volunteered to help Carolina negotiate with foreign publishers, and vouched for his integrity. The reason for lack of domestic royalties, he said, was due to the poor sales of all but her first book. Apparently her Brazilian publisher deducted its losses on the subsequent books from the royalties due her for *Quarto*.

50. Audálio Dantas, quoted in Penteado, "Carolina, vítima ou louca?" 31.
51. There is no evidence, however, that she died under these circumstances.
52. *O Globo* (Rio de Janeiro), February 14, 1977, archived at *O Globo*.
53. This, of course, was not true. She did not die "as poor as she had been" earlier.
54. Alberto Buettemuller, "Carolina Maria de Jesus: A morte longe da casa de alvenaria," *Jornal do Brasil*, February 14, 1977, Caderno B, 5.
55. Anonymous quotation given to interviewers working on Carolina Maria de Jesus project, 1992, São Paulo.
56. Karen Brown, screenplay of "Passion Flower: The Story of Carolina Maria de Jesus," Los Angeles, 1991, 122.
57. *O Globo* (Rio de Janeiro), December 11, 1969, archived at *O Globo*.
58. Cited by Penteado, "Carolina, vítima ou louca?" 31.
59. "Suplemento de Leitura" (São Paulo: Ed. Ática, 1993).
60. See Benedita da Silva's personal statement, "Fazer nossa história," in Frances O'Gorman, *Morro, Mulher*, 148–152.

Notes to Chapter 4

1. In another interview, Vera mentioned receiving small royalty payments from France as well.
2. Brizola and Jângo (João Goulart) were prominent leftist politicians. Goulart ascended to the presidency when Jânio Quadros resigned in 1961 but was deposed by the military in the 1964 coup. Brizola was elected governor of Rio de Janeiro in the 1980s. Adhemar de Barros was the corrupt populist politician who was mayor of São Paulo and later governor.
3. Benedito Fernando dos Santos, the bar owner in Iterlagos who had played the role of one of Carolina's children in the stage production of *Quarto* and who has maintained contact with Zé Carlos and Vera.
4. Interview, Marta Teresinha Godinho, January 18, 1993.

Notes to Chapter 5

1. Wilson Martins, "Mistificação literária," *Jornal do Brasil*, October 23, 1993, 4. The review angrily likened Dantas's discovery of Carolina's notebooks and the fanfare that went with it to James Macpherson's 1762 edition of poems "found in the mountains of Scotland" and to Mérimée's discredited "discovery" of the theatrical texts of Clara Gazul in 1825.
2. *Jornal do Brasil*, "Crítica," December 11, 1993, n.p. (clipping courtesy of Dr. Wilson Martins). A longer rebuttal appeared in *Imprensa*, 7 (January 1994): 42–43, a trade journal published in São Paulo.
3. This assertion is based on the authors' examination of the manuscript collection in the possession of Vera de Jesus Lima.
4. Paulo Dantas interview, São Paulo, February 2, 1993.
5. Dain Borges, "Intellectuals and the Forgetting of Slavery in Brazil," *Annals of Scholarship*, 11 (September 1994): 1–14.
6. See Rigoberta Menchú, *I Rigoberta Menchú*, 1. On the difference between traditional autobiography and testimonials, see Doris Sommer, "'Not Just a Personal Story': Women's *Testimonios* and the Plural Self,"in Bella Brodzki and Celeste Schenck, eds., *Life/Lines: Theorizing Women's Autobiography*

(Ithaca: Cornell University Press, 1988), 107–31.

7. See Patrícia Galvão's 1933 *Industrial Park,* (trans. Elizabeth and K. David Jackson (Lincoln: University of Nebraska Press, 1993), and the perceptive afterword by K. David Jackson, 115–53.

8. *Child of the Dark,* 43.

9. *Child of the Dark,* 67.

10. One politician who capitalized on this was Carlos Lacerda, who waged a press campaign during the early 1950s that he called the "Battle of Rio," blaming the government for failing to help the residents of Rio's fast-expanding shantytowns. See Luciano Parisse, *Favelas do Rio de Janeiro: Evolução-Sentido* (Rio de Janeiro: CENPHA, 1969), 113–20.

11. Space limitations preclude reproduction of the bulk of Carolina's writings on Getúlio Vargas. These will be discussed in Robert M. Levine's forthcoming *Measuring the Legacy of Getúlio Vargas's Social Legislation.*

12. Excerpts from the manuscript that was posthumously published, after editing, as *Diário de Bitita* (Rio de Janeiro: Nova Fronteira, 1986), courtesy of Vera Eunice de Jesus Lima.

13. For a statement of this frustration, see Marcelo Rubens Paiva, *Happy Old Year,* trans. David George (Pittsburgh: Latin American Literary Review Press, 1991), published in 1981 in Brazil as *Feliz Ano Velho* (São Paulo: Editora Brasiliense).

14. Jean-Claude Baker and Chris Chase, *Josephine: The Hungry Heart* (New York: Random House, 1993), 422–29.

15. Benedita da Silva, interview with Robert M. Levine, Gainesville, FL, April 3, 1993. See also Maria Ignez Costa Moreira, "Violência Contra a Mulher na Esfera Conjugal," in *Entre a Virtude e o Pecado* (Rio de Janeiro: Rosa dos Tempos, 1992, 169–190).

16. See Daphne Patai, *Brazilian Women Speak: Contemporary Life Stories* (New Brunswick: Rutgers University Press, 1988), 10–11.

17. See Daphne Patai, *Brazilian Women Speak,* 1–35, and Inderpal Grewal, "Autobiographic Subjects," in Inderpal Grewal and Caren Kaplan, eds., *Scattered Hegemonies,* 231–54.

18. St. Clair, translator's preface to *Child of the Dark,* 15.

19. Anna Lúcia Florisbela dos Santos, "An Everyday Story: Life in a *Favela,*" in Caipora Women's Group, *Women in Brazil* (London: Latin American Bureau, 1993), 29–31. See also "I've Suffered but I've Won Through: Maria's Story," 21–23. It is also telling that this book was published abroad but not in Brazil. See also Jane S. Jaquette, ed., *The Women's Movement in Latin America,* 2nd ed. (Boulder, CO: Westview Press, 1994).

20. See Michael George Hanchard, *Orpheus and Power* (Princeton: Princeton University Press, 1994); George Reid Andrews, *Blacks and Whites in Brazil* (Madison: University of Wisconsin Press, 1991).

21. Myron U and Bill I, in New York *Times,* October 10, 1993, 18.

22. This was not unlike the way that in communist-bloc countries for decades Hitler's victims were described as "socialists" or "anti-fascists," never as Jews. Vera de Jesus, in a chat at her house showing her mother's tattered archive, mentioned that some years ago she had been approached by people who wanted to donate her mother's papers and other memorabilia to a new

museum and cultural center, Casa do Negro, being planned for downtown São Paulo. But nothing ever came of the museum project, and Vera held on to her papers. In 1995, however, the authors arranged for all of Carolina's archive as well as Dantas's to be microfilmed by the U.S. Library of Congress. This project is currently underway. Included will be thirty-six unpublished notebooks of Carolina's.

23. See Dabre A. Caatillo, "Rosario Castellanos: 'Ashes without a Face'," in Sidonie Smith and Julia Watson, eds., *De/Colonizing the Subject: The Politics of Gender in Women's Autobiography* (Minneapolis: University of Minnesota Press, 1992), 242–69, esp. 245.

24. "Beti," quoted in O'Gorman, *Morro, Mulher*, 13.

25. Jane Maguire Abrams, in *Southern Changes*, referring to Elizabeth Kytle, *Willie Mae* (Athens, GA: University of Georgia Press, 1994), a first-person account of the life of a black domestic.

26. This sentiment still held fast a generation after Carolina's diary was published. See the statement, "Sofrer e Calar," by "Flávia," in O'Gorman, *Morro, Mulher*, 21.

27. The authors gratefully acknowledge the insights of Lyman Johnson for his observations about ways to interpret Carolina's life story.

Index

Alto de Santana. *See* Santana

Alves, Editora Francisco: book contract for diary, 52; as publisher of Carolina's diary, 8, 45, 71, 83–85, 105

Amado, Jorge: author of *Gabriela, Cravo e Canela,* 69; competes with Carolina, 68–69; praises her diary, 74

Araújo, Emílio Silva. *See* Silva Araújo, Emílio

Arraes, Miguel, 59, 71

B

Bahians: as objects of racial prejudice, 40; scorned by Carolina, 99

Baker, Josephine, 140

Barros, Adhemar de, 16, 125; chided by Carolina, 43; identified, 156 n. 2; relationship with Carolina, 117, 126, 138; supported by Carolina, 65; and Zé Carlos, 96

Bitita: as Carolina's childhood nickname, 27. *See also Diário de Bitita*

Black Orpheus, 90

Brand, Humberto, 31–32

Brizola, Leonel, 57; and Carolina, 71, 126; identified, 156, n. 2; and wife (Dona Neuza), 57–58

C

caboclos: Carolina disparaged as, 80; term defined, 29

Câmara, Archbishop Dom Helder, 56, 65, 71

Canindé favela, 14, 78, 95, 99–100, 106, 111, 117, 136; Carolina builds shack in, 37–39, 71, 122; Audálio Dantas goes to write about, 44; difficulty of having a "normal" life in, 133; ethnic diversity of residents, 40; moving day from, 53, 105; one of less than a dozen favelas in São Paulo, 93; political campaigns in, 65; samba written about, 60; torn down, 14, 93; on map, 22; photographs of, 22, 48

"Carolinas": members of Guarujá Women's Association, xii, 13, 90–91. *See also* Guarujá Women's Association

Casa de Alvenaria, 61, 71–72, 106, 119; publication history of, 71, 73; translations of, 73; no copy owned by Carolina, 81; as symbol, 138

Castro, Lélio de: as business manager of Editora Francisco Alves, 45

Child of the Dark: editor praises diary, 74; published in U.S., 6, 67, 79; used in college classes, 3, 7, 12, 19–20. *See also Quarto de Despejo*

Clíris (novel), 42

Cruzeiro, O, 45, 109

Cunha, Euclydes da, 10, 82

D

Dantas, Audálio: accused of literary mystification, 135; accuses Carolina of deception, 77; accuses Carolina of squandering her income on men, 86;